BEST FOOT
FORWARD

BEST FOOT FORWARD

A guide to planning and enjoying walks in Britain

Anthony Burton

AURUM PRESS

First published 1998 by Aurum Press Ltd, 25 Bedford Avenue, London WC1B 3AT
Text and photographs copyright © Anthony Burton 1998

Anthony Burton hereby asserts his moral right to be identified as the author of this work

Map on pages 22-3 reproduced from Ordnance Survey 1:50 000 Landranger 198 Brighton and the
Downs map; map on pages 30-1 reproduced from Ordnance Survey 1:25 000 Explorer 17 South
Downs Way, Steyning to Newhaven map; with the permission of The Controller of Her Majesty's
Stationery Office © Crown copyright License Number 43453U

A catalogue record for this book is available from the British Library.

ISBN 185410 558 2

Book design by Robert Updegraff
Printed and bound in Italy by Printer Trento srl

Frontispiece Invitation to the walk: canal towpath near Llangollen.

CONTENTS

Highland wilderness in Gleann Easan Biorach, Arran.

Introduction

Like many who enjoy going out into the countryside, I began walking when I was still at school. In those days it often seemed more important to clock up the miles than to pause and look around, and when I turned from hill-walking to rock-climbing, the few inches of rock in front of my nose demanded all my attention. All that has changed, partly because with maturity I began to appreciate that there was a good deal to be said for taking time to view the landscape through which I walked – to sit on a rock beside a stream and watch the bustle of the dippers or simply to pause and try to take in the immense variety of a distant view. However, the turning point in my personal approach to the countryside can be pinpointed with greater accuracy: it occurred on the day I first picked up a copy of W. G. Hoskins' seminal work, *The Making of the English Landscape*. The landscape stopped being just scenery and became a part of a far more complex, and infinitely more interesting, story of change. My own preoccupations with transport and industrial history fitted comfortably into this newly discovered way of seeing the countryside through which I walked.

One aim of this book is to try and share with the reader my own absolute conviction that understanding something of the history of the landscape adds immensely to the pleasures of a country walk. But that is only part of it. Over the last few years I have spent a great deal of time devising walks and writing them up for others; walks long and short, walks in the mountains and walks in the valleys. And, at the risk of writing myself out of a job, I have become convinced that the pleasures of making a walk of one's own far outweigh those of following someone else's instructions – when the walk works, that is. So the other aim of this book is not to tell the reader where to go, but to give hints and suggestions as to the sort of factors that need to be considered in planning a walk.

These two aspects of this book – encouraging an interest in landscape history and showing how to plan an enjoyable walk – have obvious connections. The first thing a publisher tends to ask an author to consider when describing a walk is one or more 'points of interest'. But while it is certainly no bad thing in planning to have a few highlights in mind, there is a

A quiet time for contemplation at Hartland Quay, Devon.

danger that the bits in between are thought of as just that, the necessary but rather dull linking passages. What I hope to show over the following pages is that once you get into the habit of looking with care, and knowing what you are looking at, almost everything becomes of interest.

What I am emphatically not trying to do is turn every walk into some kind of outdoor geography or history lesson – I have too many memories of terrible, tedious school nature walks for that. My aim is really very much simpler. I want everyone to get more pleasure out of walking, by feeling

confident that they can happily set off on their very own walks and discover that the countryside of Britain is a place of infinite variety and endless fascination – endless, because once you develop an interest you will find, as I have found, that for every question that is answered a dozen more will spring up. On a rough calculation, I have over the years devised and written up some 200 walks, and I feel that I have hardly begun. If at the end of this book, the reader feels like heading off to find 200 more then I shall feel that this has been a job well done.

A footpath curls across the hills of the South Downs.

Chapter 1
GETTING READY

'Going for a walk' is a phrase that covers anything from taking out the dogs for a run to a long-distance trek of a hundred miles or more. For walking the dog, little is strictly necessary apart from the leash: those setting out on longer routes need to be equipped for the task. All equipment has to be judged against one or both of the following criteria: does it make the walker more comfortable? Does it add to safety?

The most important part of the body as far as the walker is concerned is the part that takes all the weight: the foot. Nothing ruins a walk more than wet, sore and blistered feet; nothing is more dangerous than slippery soles on wet rocks. There are walking shoes, walking boots and these days, walking sandals, all of which will normally be fitted with compressed rubber patterned soles, usually the type known as Vibram. These are all excellent at providing a good grip – it hardly needs saying that anything with a smooth sole is useless, and a leather sole a great deal worse than useless. Many people whose walking is limited to footpaths and fields find shoes perfectly adequate, but they are not really suitable for the hills. Here the boot, with its protection for the ankle, is essential. The sandal is very popular, but not as an all-weather, all-season form of footwear. I did once meet a lady along the coast-to-coast Scottish route, the Southern Upland Way, attempting the 200-plus miles (320 km) in sandals. Her joy in finding the cool air blowing across bare skin was being steadily diminished as more and more of the skin disappeared under sticky plasters. The other option which many take is the ubiquitous 'trainer', but this is strictly a fair-weather shoe; so the majority of walkers opt for boots. The matter does not quite end there, for boots come in many different varieties and at many different prices. It is not strictly true to say the higher the price the better the value, but it is true that a very cheap boot is seldom worth buying. The two main options are boots with traditional leather uppers and those made of a 'breathing' fabric, such as Gortex. There are no rules here, and it is very much down to personal preference – even the author can offer no real help, having a pair of each. In general, the fabric boot will offer total water-proofing, while leather withstands almost everything, with the exception of long, wet grass. The fabric boot tends to be lighter, but not as long-lasting as the leather. Those who are buying for the first time should go to a good, specialist shop that can offer sound advice but in the end the main aim is to find the boot that suits your foot. And do remember to wear walking socks of the type you will be using when trying the boot on.

Boots do vary in weight depending on the use to which they are to be put, from the heavy, often very rigidly-soled mountain boot to the lightweight. Check the manufacturer's specification to make sure that you get a boot that suits your needs. A good pair of boots will last for years, and one is very reluctant to say goodbye. I have a pair of leather boots which have covered many hundreds of miles, and it was only with the greatest reluctance that I had to admit their time had come. Before setting out for a long walk in new boots, check what water-proofing is needed, and break them in gently with a few short strolls.

Clothing is very much a matter of personal preference, but there is one golden rule. Whatever you wear when you set out on a walk, always have clothing that will be appropriate for the weather that it is possible to meet – not just likely, but possible. A brilliantly hot, summer day can erupt into a thunderstorm resulting in an absolute deluge. If the sun is lost behind winter clouds, the drop in temperature can be dramatic, and changes in the terrain can produce equally startling contrasts. In early spring, for example, tourists may wander round the foot of Snowdon in shorts and tee shirts, while at the summit there are sub-zero temperatures and the paths are encased in ice.

There are certain materials which are altogether unsuitable for walking – jeans, for example, become quite horribly heavy and waterlogged in the rain. What is essential is to have genuine weather-proof clothing. The choice is immense. Some, like myself, favour fleece jackets which are good year-round wear and are shower-proof: the waterproofs stay in the rucksack unless wet weather has really set in. Others prefer the more traditional anorak. There are those who buy weather-proof trousers of breathing fabric: others prefer light-weight garments and over-trousers for foul days. Sun hats, rain hats, anorak hoods, woolly hats – all have their champions. Again it is a question of finding clothing that is suitable for walking – which means allowing flexibility – and which is comfortable for the wearer. There are those who wear gaiters, others knee breeches – and some who opt for trousers stuck in socks. The one thing that has to be said is that good clothing makes for enjoyable walking – and can save your life. Each year there are those who set out for wild country in bad weather with inappropriate clothing and then, if things go wrong, run a real risk of dying of hypothermia.

What equipment you choose to carry again depends on the type of walk. A small rucksack is all that is needed for a day's outing, a large rucksack for long walks and a bigger one still for those who camp out *en route*. A frame rucksack with waist straps – and chest straps if really large loads are carried – is far the most comfortable to carry. A certain amount of basic equipment should always be carried – a simple first aid kit, which does not mean an entire medicine chest – is invaluable. Things do go wrong, and even a simple matter like having a plaster to put on a blister can make all the difference between an enjoyable walk and a miserable hobble. And if things do go seriously wrong, and an individual or a party have no choice other than staying put and waiting for rescue, then two simple pieces of equipment, a whistle and a torch will help the rescuers arrive all the sooner. At this point it is perhaps worth mentioning that rescuers will not even attempt to find you unless they know you are missing. Always make sure that someone knows where you are walking and when you expect to arrive at the end of the day.

There are two other essential items of equipment that always need to be carried – map and compass, the use of which is discussed in the next chapter. Many people carry the map folded away in a pocket, but this can be very

The swoop of downland into small, hidden valleys is one of the most appealing features of this landscape. But here, at Devil's Dyke, another feature appears: the ramparts of a hill fort.

inconvenient in bad weather. Paper and rain are not a good combination, and opening up a map on a windy day can be an interesting exercise to say the least. An alternative is the map case made of weatherproof material with a transparent plastic front. One point to note is that there is little point in having a map case if one is constantly jiggling it around. The map case is usually hung from cords, so it is generally most convenient to fold the map inside so that the route goes from the top to the bottom of the case. That way, when you hold it up, the path on the map is aligned with the path on the ground.

A recent, and very popular, addition to the walker's equipment is the walking pole, made of lightweight alloy and looking very like a ski-pole. Essentially it serves the same function as the old fashioned walking stick, but many walkers use them in pairs. They are particularly useful in easing the way uphill and providing stability when going down steep slopes and they can help keep the feet dry by providing support when crossing streams.

Fully equipped, the walker is ready to go, but there is one other item that needs to be in first-class order, the human body. Those who are not used to walking over long distances cannot expect to go straight out and walk 25 miles (40 km) a day over the hills for a week. It is best to build up stamina gradually – and not to worry if you find that there is a limit to what you can do. There are those who regard miles covered in a day as the only test of a good outing, and that is their choice – even if it is not a choice some of us care to make. The object of walking is pleasure and satisfaction. True, there is a real satisfaction in overcoming obstacles and there is nothing wrong with feeling tired at the end of a day, but there is a limit. No-one should feel compelled to push themselves to the point of exhaustion, and there is not much to be said for walking so far one day that you can scarcely move on the next. The sensible approach is to start with short easy walks and gradually increase length and difficulty until you find your own limits.

Long walks present their own problems of which the most obvious is that the walker needs somewhere to stay at night. Those who camp out have great freedom, but others must hunt out hostels, bed and breakfasts, inns or hotels. One can trust to luck but as it is the nature of long-distance walks that they are generally chosen to include as much open country and as few urban areas as possible, this is not always a good idea. Planning and booking ahead is generally advisable. Accommodation lists are published for most of the established long-distance walks and details can generally be found in walk guides or obtained from tourist information centres. Sometimes stops are few and far between, and it is a good general rule to underestimate rather than overestimate the distance you are prepared to walk in a day. What is true of accommodation is equally true of places to eat. There will be days when nothing is available at all and, in any case, one has to be prepared for things going wrong. The first essential is to have something to drink in the rucksack – and ordinary tap water is as good as anything – and it is a good idea to top up the water bottle whenever the chance appears. There are a number of good, high energy food bars available these days, light to carry, not taking up much space but full of nutrients. They can be bought from walking shops and many wholefood shops.

It is all too easy when offering advice to give the impression that every walker should always set off prepared for something between a polar expedition and a traverse of the Himalayas. Like all 'rules' these have to be applied with commonsense, and if an individual decides to break them that choice is open. Many guide books, for example, suggest that long walks should always be undertaken by groups of at least three, so that in the case of injury there is one to stay with the victim and a third to go for help. This is very sound thinking, but over the last few years I have walked many hundreds of miles with no companions other than those met by chance along the way. I am aware of the risks but make a deliberate choice, whilst doing everything sensible to minimise those risks. These few notes are suggestions to those taking up serious walking for the first time, intended to ensure that all goes well and that the experience is as enjoyable as possible. But by far the most important factor in making for enjoyment is the nature of the walk itself, which is the subject of the rest of this book.

A typically wayward Devon lane.

Chapter 2

THE MAP

> There are certain sheets of the one-inch Ordnance Survey
> map which one can sit down and read like a book for an hour
> on end, with growing pleasure and imaginative excitement.
>
> W.G. Hoskins, *The Making of the English Landscape*

This quotation from Hoskins might seem a little bizarre to those who think of maps as no more than handy devices for helping you to find the way from one place to the next. But those who start devising their own walks will invariably find themselves infected with the same enthusiasm. The map becomes much more than a flat sheet of paper with lines indicating paths. It grows in the mind into a real, three-dimensional landscape – one could even say into a four-dimensional landscape, for the history of the land can be read as well as its present form. This is particularly true of maps of Britain, where the Ordnance Survey have been developing and perfecting the art of map-making for more than two hundred years. So, before turning to look at the actual map, how it is used and the story it has to tell, it is worth pausing for a moment to look at a very brief, potted history of the Ordnance Survey, which will help to put the whole subject into context, and show just how much progress has been made since the eighteenth century.

It all began with the Jacobite Rebellion of 1745, when the English troops in Scotland found themselves severely handicapped by a lack of good maps. Major-General William Roy took on the task of providing a hand-drawn map of the Highlands to a scale of 1 inch to 1000 yards (1:36 000), showing the terrain and the main lines of communication. Then he set about creating what he hoped would be a more scientific series of maps of Britain by the technique known as triangulation. This involved setting up an accurately measured base-line – in this case on Hounslow Heath, the site of what is now Heathrow Airport. A distant object was chosen and theodolites were set up at each end of the base-line. The theodolite is essentially a telescope mounted in a graduated circle, so that angles can be read. An imaginary triangle can thus be created, with length of the base-line and the angles between it and each of the other two sides accurately measured. This fixes the position of the third point and establishes the length of two new base lines. And so the process can be

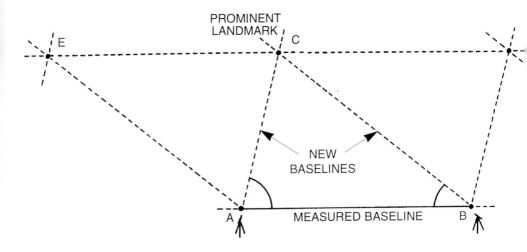

Triangulation Using a theodolite, bearings on a prominent landmark, C, are taken from the ends of a measured baseline at A and B. This establishes the position of C, and using simple trigonometry the lengths of the two new baselines, A-C and B-C, can be established. Two more triangles can then be constructed with their apexes at E and F.

continued. Roy's theodolite was a splendid affair by Ramsden, the leading instrument maker of the day, and was mounted on a three-foot circle. Progress was, however, slow and official interest limited. Things moved with all the deliberation for which governments are famous, and it was not until 1791 that the Ordnance Survey was actually founded. It was, as the name suggests, still very much concerned with the needs of the military, and a certain urgency was injected into proceedings by the growing threat of invasion from France. As Kent was the likeliest area to be attacked, it was Kent that was first mapped. In 1801 a map of the county was produced at a scale of one inch to the mile (approximately 1:63 000) – a scale that was to be closely identified with the Ordnance Survey for nearly two hundred years. But as the threat of war on British soil receded, so the Ordnance Survey found itself increasingly meeting the general public's demand for good, clear maps. The one-inch range of maps was extended to cover the whole country and became generally available.

In 1820 when Thomas Colby was appointed Director of the Ordnance Survey, cartography moved rapidly forward. In 1825 he began mapping the whole of Ireland on a scale of six-inches to the mile. He set out a base-line on flat land beside Lough Foyle. It was eight miles long, and when Colby's base was recently remeasured using the latest electronic equipment, it was found to be out by only one inch over the entire length – an extraordinarily small error of just 1 in 500,000. He was equally determined to authenticate the name of every town, river, lake, stream and even large buildings – all recorded in the official Name Book. Ever since his day, the OS maps have been recognised as the final authority in all matters of place names. Now maps were engraved instead of being drawn by hand by a whole series of specialists, assuring the finest of lines and the greatest accuracy. By mid-century the maps had become both more attractive and clearer with the introduction of colour. Today we take colour printing for granted, but back in 1855 the Ordnance Survey proudly reported that they had a 'number of boys from 13 to 14 years of age, taught to colour these large maps; they are paid from 6d to 1s a day' (2½ – 5p in today's money).

In the early 1900s triangulation techniques were improved, and the position of 20,000 points accurately recorded, 6,500 of which were marked by concrete pillars – the familiar 'trig points'. Aerial surveys have added immensely to the accuracy of mapping, and a new system based on satellites – the Global Positioning System – has done even more. The computer age has brought in digitalisation, and this has made regular updating of maps far easier. But it is not just technology that has changed.

In the twentieth century, the move was made to market the one-inch map as 'The Complete Guide to the Countryside', with walkers, cyclists and the growing number of motorists heading for a day out in the country very much in mind. The one-inch was eventually replaced by the Landranger 1:50 000 series giving a better scale of roughly 1¼ inches to the mile, or precisely 2 centimetres to the kilometre. To those were added the 1:25 000 series, aptly named Pathfinder, for with one of these in hand and the ability to use it, the walker can indeed be sure of finding the right path. The second Landranger series, representing a complete revision covering the whole country was completed in 1987 and the revision of the Pathfinders was completed in 1989. In recent years, the Pathfinders have been increasingly replaced by Explorer and Outdoor Leisure Maps to the same scale, but covering a far greater area – ten different Pathfinders, for example, would have been needed to cover the area represented on the Outdoor Leisure Maps of Exmoor. The Outdoor Leisure series cover popular tourist areas such as the National Parks, and Explorers are steadily replacing Pathfinders in a planned programme that started with the South Coast and will steadily move further north. But that will still leave well over a thousand Pathfinders in use at the beginning of the next century. So it is still convenient for the sake of example to refer to all 1:25 000 maps as Pathfinders.

Scale is not the only difference between Landrangers and Pathfinders. There are also mapping differences, in particular the system for marking rights of way – red on the Landranger, green on the Pathfinder. Landrangers and Pathfinders are the basic tools for planning the walk in the study and for walking the route itself on the ground. There are other maps available, which can be of considerable interest. I regularly turn to the Ordnance Survey's Ancient Britain map, and a good geological map is invaluable in understanding the different forms that the landscape takes. These are worth having, but are not essential in the way that Pathfinders and Landrangers are, and it is the latter we shall now be looking at in more detail. Quite the best way of learning about maps is to use them, and I have selected one small area of the country to use as an example – but first a simple, basic explanation of map references.

The first essential in discussing a map is to make sure that everyone is talking about the same thing or, more specifically, the same place. Any point on an OS map can be accurately identified in terms of its grid reference. The maps I have chosen as an example are Landranger 198 Brighton and the Downs and Explorer 17 South Downs Way, Steyning to Newhaven, which includes the area previously covered by Pathfinder 1288 Burgess Hill. Suppose I want to refer the reader to a particular point of interest. Poynings Church, for example.

It would be very tedious to have to spend an age searching the entire map to find it – quoting a grid reference reduces the time required to a few seconds. The whole of Britain is covered by a mapping grid. The large units are 100,000 metre squares, identified by letters printed at the top and bottom corners of the map. The top, northern part of Landranger 198 falls in square TQ, the lower southern section in TV. Poynings is in the north so the reference begins TQ.

These large lettered squares are subdivided into kilometre squares, with the dividing lines numbered 1 to 100 west to east and 1 to 100 south to north. Grid references give 'eastings', the number of the line to the left, or west, of the point to be described, first. In this case the north-south line to the left of Poynings is 26. This is followed by the 'northing', the number of the east-west line below the point to be identified, in this case 12. This defines the one-kilometre square in which the church can be found as TQ2612. Even greater accuracy can be achieved by estimating tenths along the square's edges. The church is roughly ⁵⁄₁₀ of the way between the vertical lines 26 and 27 and ¹⁄₁₀ of the way between the horizontal lines 12 and 13, giving a complete grid reference of TQ265121. This is a unique grid reference for Britain, but where, as here, one specific map is being discussed, it is not necessary to quote the letters. It remains, however, a useful guide when one finds references in older books written when the Landrangers were still one inch to the mile maps and differently numbered – for the grid reference remains the same.

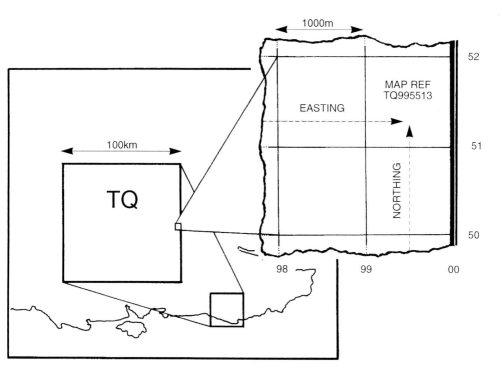

Map references The one shown here is for a woodland path in Kent. The letters, TQ, identify the 100-km square within which the position lies. The six numbers which follow, the 'eastings' and the 'northing', locate it to within 100 metres on both co-ordinates.

This process seems tedious when written out at length, but in practice is simple and very, very useful. So now, having a system that ensures writer and reader are looking at the same places, we can turn to the much more interesting subject of the maps themselves.

The Landranger (pages 22-3) is the obvious starting point if you wish to gain an overall view of the area, which in this case divides into three bands. To the south is the coastal strip, which offers very little of interest to the prospective walker, being built up all the way from Worthing in the west to Seaford in the east. Immediately inland are the South Downs, rising to a height of over 600 feet (200 metres). Here the contour lines, each of which indicates a 10-metre change in altitude, squirm and wriggle all over the map, suggesting a very irregular, undulating landscape. Even without being able to interpret the lines at first glance, the names tell the same story; and what enticing names they are: Thundersbarrow Hill stands above Bushy Bottom while Cockroost Hill lords it over lowly Skeleton Hovel. The southern edge of the Downs consists of more or less gentle slopes running down to the sea, but at the northern

escarpment the contours cluster together, crowding in on each other as the land swoops down to the valley floor. The only real breaks in this pattern are created by rivers such as the Adur forcing their way through to the sea. What this area promises is interesting walking with constantly changing views, and possibly a few strenuous uphill slogs thrown in for good measure.

To the north, the picture changes completely. This is mostly low-lying land, with widely separated contours. Whereas the Downs have few roads, no settlements larger than isolated farms, and no streams or rivers other than the Adur and the Ouse, here is a complex pattern of roads and lanes, towns and villages, a landscape criss-crossed by rivers and streams and patched with woodland. One expects to find paths across farmland occasionally diving into the woods, with no steep climbs, but without the panoramic views and the sense of wide, open spaces that are promised by the Downs. On the other hand, the map is crowded with features which promise to be of considerable interest. A closer look gives some idea of the diversity of the land. There are, for example, many of the stippled grey areas that indicate parkland, usually associated with some grand house. At Chestham Park (2117) a path runs right through the middle of the park, passing close by the house itself.

The more one studies the map, the more different patterns begin to emerge. It soon becomes clear that the story told by the contour lines, indicating a fundamental change in the geological patterns of the region, is mirrored by a different story of the way in which man too has imposed a pattern on the land. A glance at the geological map confirms what one could deduce: an area of underlying chalk forming the Downs, and heavy clays in the lowlands. Today, the downland is largely open with few habitations, but there are also marks all over the map suggesting that this was once a most favoured area. The gothic script used to indicate antiquities is liberally spattered across this region, showing old field systems, hill forts and the more enigmatic 'tumuli'. The map even hints at how this may have come about. All those green patches in the lowland area indicating woodland are so widely distributed that one would guess, quite rightly, that the whole area was once densely forested. For people equipped with only primitive tools this would have been a daunting sight; and even when woods were cleared the heavy, cloying soil would have been difficult to work. On the uplands, however, the chalk was covered by a thin layer of light soil, an altogether more appealing prospect. Walkers with a special interest in the ancient world will find the Downs full of interest.

Moving forward in time, evidence of settlement in the lowland region begins to appear, first in the form of Roman roads sweeping across the map, if not always in the proverbial straight lines: the road through what is now Bedlam Street (2815), for example, makes a quite abrupt change in direction.The later medieval world is hinted at by the presence of castles and moated dwellings and in the many names of manors and manor farms. So here we have a picture of woodland being cleared and a rich agricultural land being created by heavy ploughs. Even the most cursory glance has revealed the outlines of a complex story and has hinted at the possibility of creating walks that might be appealing in the traditional sense of traversing attractive countryside and which might also incorporate a large number of features of interest.

Which features are highlighted can be a matter of personal preference, and sometimes one interest can lead on to others. Those whose main interest is in the natural world might be drawn to the headquarters of the Sussex Wildlife Trust at Woods Mill (218137) where they will find a rich diversity of habitats with managed woodland which in spring sparkles with bluebells and primroses, lake and marshland where one can watch the statuesque heron or catch the brief, startling blue flash of a kingfisher skimming the water. Nature reserves are invariably accessible by footpath and usually provide first class information on the habitat and its wildlife. This makes them particularly valuable for those who have just begun bird watching or are starting to take an interest in plant or insect life. It is, of course, perfectly possible to walk the country, seeing the wildlife, listening to the cries of the birds without being able to indentify anything – the lark will not sing any sweeter for being named. But, as with so many subjects, the more one learns the more interested one becomes – and the more one realises just how much there is to know – sadly, far too much for a book of this kind. There is, however, no shortage of specialist books covering the different aspects of the natural world.

Woods Mill itself is an eighteenth-century water mill originally used for grinding corn, so perhaps one might be tempted to see other ways in which man has adapted natural forces for his own use. At Clayton (3013) there are symbols for not one but two windmills, a rare sight in Britain. But this is not the only place of interest here. The London to Brighton railway dives through the hill in a 1¼ mile (2 km) long tunnel, an achievement which the company's architect David Mocatta celebrated with an elaborate mock-medieval portal, all battlements and arrow slits. Railways have their own addicts, and disused lines can be both interesting and provide agreeably level footpaths, as does a large part of the former London and Brighton South Coast Railway passing by Henfield (2015). One could with very little trouble, look at this one map and think up ideas for at least half a dozen walks, each of which would have its own distinct character. So the planner has to make a few decisions about what sort of walk he is looking to make.

For those who want a really long walk taking several days, two long-distance trails feature on this map – the well-known South Downs Way and the Sussex Border Path. Such routes will have been carefully planned, with discus-

Clayton windmills, Jack and Jill. Jill is a post-mill in which the whole housing turns on a central post. Jack has his sails mounted on a rotating cap at the top of the tower.

sions involving everyone from planning authorities to walkers' representatives. In general routes will have been chosen to provide access to the very best of local scenery and to incorporate as many points of interest as possible. It is fair to say that it would be extremely difficult to think of a better introduction to the Downland of South East England than that offered by the South Downs Way. And what is true of this one particular path is equally true of more than forty long-distance trails and footpaths in the British Isles. They have the added advantages that they are well maintained with stiles and gates in good order, footpaths kept clear of obstructions and, in most cases, well waymarked – though it would not be a good idea to set off for a hundred-mile trek relying on signposts to point you in the right direction all along the way. But because they are reliable, one can use even a short section in fair confidence of meeting no real problems. Not everyone likes to rely on others to choose a route – and a great deal of route choosing goes on these days. Local paths have proliferated, and it is not unusual for a walker to arrive at a gate with yellow arrows, blue arrows, red arrows all pointing in different ways for different paths.

Walkers on the South Downs Way. This is typical of the superb countryside through which the Way passes with the white gleam of chalk paths contrasting with the rounded greenness of the hills.

Beacon Hill, South Downs. A hill fort and earthworks provide interest of one sort, while the walk along the escarpment edge gives wide views over the Rother valley.

Unless one is armed with a bag full of leaflets it can be more confusing than helpful: which is one good reason for going back to basics and making one's own route from the map.

For the present, let us assume that we are thinking of a day's walk that will take in something of the character of both upland and lowland. Before planning any walk there is one very obvious question that needs to be answered – how long is it to be? In general, it is best to think in terms of time rather than distance – all day, an afternoon, a couple of hours or whatever, then plan the walk, taking account of the terrain. A useful guide is Naismith's Rule which says that the average walker covers a kilometre in a quarter of an hour on the flat, but that 4 minutes need to be added for every 30 metres climbed. It should be stressed that this is an average rate, and times will vary with many factors from the state of the weather to the fitness of the individual. It is worth getting used to thinking metric, because metric units are the ones that can be taken directly from the map – even if you still proudly announce at the end of the day that you have just walked 20 miles!

Should walks be circular or linear? The advantages of the circular walk are self-evident, but linear walks should not be ruled out. At times public transport can be used to return to the start, but there is nothing wrong with spending half the allotted time walking one way and then turning round and coming back. It is surprising how different a walk can seem going in the opposite direction. Turning back to our Landranger map, a likely area for a walk might be centred on the little village of Fulking (2411). To the south, the Downs rise in a steep escarpment, with a number of features, ranging from a Norman motte and bailey to an Iron Age hill fort. Down below in the valley there are no busy main roads, just a gentle landscape with clumps of woodland and wandering streams. To get a clearer picture we can now turn to the Pathfinder map (pages 30-1).

The most obvious change at the 1:25 000 scale is the appearance of field boundaries. The divisions at the top of the Downs form large enclosures, and the track that runs close to the edge is scarcely interrupted by walls or fences. There are subtle variations in the terrain. At Perching Hill summit (244109) there is a view down over folded grassland, but then the track to the east dips slightly before climbing again to run above a steep escarpment with lots of scrubby bushes and trees, shown by the map symbols. It eventually arrives at a promontory with a deep hollow to the south, known as Devil's Dyke. The nature of the land made this an ideal defensible position for the Iron Age people who settled here before the Roman invasion. They improved on the natural defences provided by the steep slopes by creating a massive bank and ditch across the narrow neck of the promontory, and building minor earthworks around the gently sloping northern edge – all of which can be seen on the map.

These are all very attractive features, and one can be quite confident that a walk along the escarpment will be an enjoyable experience. There are many paths linking the Downs with the valley floor, so decisions on the next part of the route depend on how much of the upper path is to be included, whether the walker favours a steep but short or gentle but long ascent and descent, and what should be included in the lower part of the walk. The village of Fulking itself looks interesting. Its origins can be surmised from the springs shown on the map. The Downs have for many centuries been used for grazing sheep, and at shearing time they had to be gathered together and washed ready for the cutting of the fleeces. Today, the springs emerge through an ornate ceramic surround next to the aptly named Shepherd and Dog pub. The village shows a typical pattern of houses spread down the main street, with long plots running down to a back lane. A traditional pattern holds out promise of traditional buildings and the visitor will not be disappointed. In an area lacking good building stone, many of the cottages are wooden framed and roofed with thatch. So Fulking can make a case for being visited on a walk.

Whereas Fulking appears as a regularly organised village, Poynings to the east is diffuse with no obvious centre, but it is Poynings not Fulking which has the extra status of a church. In fact the village is named after the wealthy Poynings family who held the manor for three centuries. A visit to the church should reveal just how generous they were in their patronage. They were clearly major landowners whose influence spread at least as far as Poynings Grange Farm (258131). Poynings looks to be another point to feature on a walk. We are now getting near to the actual planning stage, and all that has to be decided is the length of time to be out. Just as an exercise, let us choose a modest afternoon's walk – an outing of around 3 hours. Now is the time to apply Naismith's rule. The maximum climb from the valley is roughly 150 metres, so 20 minutes has to be taken off the 3 hours to allow for that, and on a walk like this, with much to see, time also has to be allowed for looking at things and places, so why not allow a generous hour to take account of everything. That leaves a modest walk of around 8 km – about 5 miles – which happily can be laid out taking in all our points of interest. A route could start by the pub in Fulking and head uphill via the long dog leg to the east. From the

The South Downs escarpment edge above Fulking. The photograph covers much of the area shown on the map on pages 30-31, and the reader should be able to compare the two and identify specific features.

top of the hill, head east to go through the middle of the Devil's Dyke fort, out through the eastern ramparts and downhill to Poynings church. From here a footpath leads north to a crossroads. Then a little lane leads to Grange Lodge Cottages, and a path which does a great circuit via Poynings Grange Farm and Brook House and back to Fulking.

Having decided on the general pattern, it is always a good idea to draw a route on the map in pencil, so that it can be measured. You can guess the distance from the kilometre squares, measure it using a piece of string or, best of all, use a map wheel. This is just a miniature version of the wheel on a stick used for measuring roads. In this case, the tiny wheel is run along the route and the distance read off the dial – very simple. In this case the walk works out at the length we were looking for – 7 to 8 km. This, of course, is just one route – alternatives of the same length could be devised, as well as shorter or longer versions.

One longer version that might tempt me would include a visit to Newtimber Place (269138) because it represents a mystery. The map shows a considerable moated property, with an old rectory and a church to the south. But where is the village? Who went to the church? What I would hope to find would be a lot of humps and hollows in the surrounding fields, the remains of a village depopulated, perhaps, in late medieval times. Or perhaps the village was cleared for the 'new timber'. The map hints at a story – a walk might supply at least part of the plot.

Sitting at home planning walks and drawing maps is actually a very pleasant occupation, but to complete the process means getting out of the house and into the country. Now new skills come into play, for the neat lines drawn on the map have to be made to match the complex reality found on the ground. The simplest part of this route would seem to be the track along the edge of the Downs, above the escarpment. And so it is. Many of the upland paths are so well used that the turf and topsoil have worn away, leaving a strip of exposed chalk that gleams brilliant white in the sun, but turns to slithery, greasy grey in the wet. Route finding in the valley can be altogether more complex, and it is here that the Pathfinder proves its worth. The majority of the paths go through farmland, and it is important that walkers keep to the right of way. The path may be a bold green line on the map, but may be a good deal less obvious on the ground. What the map clearly shows is the path's position in relation to field boundaries. Heading north from Poyning, for example, the path heads diagonally across a field – avoiding the wet ground round the springs – and then crosses into the adjoining field. Between Poynings Grange Farm and Brook House, the path stays to the north of the fence or hedge, and then crosses to the other side. None of this is shown on the Landranger.

This may make route-finding seem simplicity itself, but there are snares in plenty. Field boundaries are not set for all time, and the map gives no indication of how they will appear on the ground – solid stone wall, high hedge, or narrow strands of wire. Some hedges may have been grubbed up, leaving little if any trace on the ground. This is very common, particularly in areas such as East Anglia. In other cases new fences may have been added – and the older the last major revision date on the map, the more changes there are likely to be on the ground. Paths that seem clear on the map can appear confusing on the ground, and what seemed a simple task at the start of the day can become a daunting challenge when mist creeps over the land or clouds drop over the hills. On these occasions there is only one answer to route finding: the compass.

It may seem slightly absurd to think of carrying a compass on a simple country walk, but there are days when one is glad of its presence, even in areas such as this. I remember taking what should have been a simple walk at the eastern end of the South Downs above the Seven Sisters cliffs when a sea fog rolled in and obliterated everything from view in just a few minutes. It is astonishing how quickly one's sense of direction is lost when every landmark disappears from view – and somewhat unnerving when heading the wrong way might lead straight to a cliff edge. There was no real danger of plunging into the sea, but there was a prospect of spending a great deal of time wandering around trying to find my way back to the start. But with map and compass I was able to follow the planned route quite accurately. On this occasion the worst I would have suffered would have been the inconvenience of a wearisome detour, but in truly wild country the penalties for getting lost can be severe. A compass is an essential for any serious walker, and scarcely less valuable for the not so serious – provided the owner knows how to use it.

A simple compass, with nothing more complex than a needle pointing north has its uses – at least you can tell which way you are facing, but it is worth making a modest investment in something a little more sophisticated. A popular choice is the Silva-type compass, set on a rectangular base plate, engraved with an arrow showing the direction of travel. There are two basic uses for the compass: the first is for orientation to identify landmarks shown on the map, the second is for finding out which way you need to go. The obvious method of orientation is to align the red end of the compass needle with north on the map: to be strictly accurate it has to be remembered that the compass points to magnetic north, while the map shows true north, but in practice this can generally be ignored. In the area we have been looking at the difference is about 1° which is not very significant.

Getting an accurate direction of travel takes a little more care; the diagram above shows the process, step by step. It sounds fiendishly complicated, but becomes easy with practice. The best thing to do is to go on a walk where directions are very obvious or which you know well and put it to the test. It is an invaluable skill to

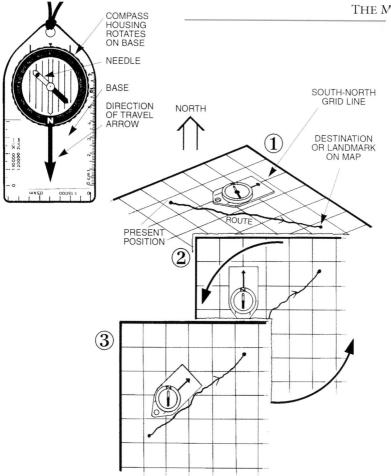

COMPASS HOUSING ROTATES ON BASE

NEEDLE

BASE

DIRECTION OF TRAVEL ARROW

NORTH

SOUTH-NORTH GRID LINE

DESTINATION OR LANDMARK ON MAP

ROUTE

PRESENT POSITION

Using a compass The compass housing is turned so that the N symbol lines up with the direction of travel arrow and the transparent base is positioned on the map so that the direction of travel arrow points north up a gridline (1). Keeping the map level, and holding the compass in position, it is turned until the compass needle points to the N; the map is now orientated (2). Finally, with the map held in position, the compass is placed so that the direction of travel arrow points along the route (or, if the route is not marked on the map, along an imaginary line joining your present position to your destination or some intermediate point on the map). Pick a landmark in the direction indicated by the arrow and head for it (3); or if you turn the compass housing so that the N aligns with the tip of the compass needle, you can also read off the compass bearing you should follow. In bad weather it may be necessary to repeat this performance at regular intervals.

master. It is, in any case, no bad thing to take an occasional glance at the compass, just to be sure that you are travelling in the right direction. One of the commonest mistakes walkers make is to be lulled into error by a very obvious track. For example, a farm track may be followed for some way, but the footpath may diverge from it and be scarcely notable. It is all too easy to keep straight on – until the compass informs you of the error of your ways.

Unexpected sightseers discovered on a country walk. These two seated figures by Henry Moore are among a number of sculptures set among the wild scenery of Glen Kiln.

Planning is essential for a good walk – but no plans are perfect. Maps are drawn at a particular time, and the landscape itself is ever changing. A whole walk can be put out of gear because a footbridge was swept away in a flood a week before; a walker might be thrown into a panic because the conifer planta-tion shown as lying across the path is nowhere in sight: it was felled a month ago. By far the most common change is the uprooted hedge, where two small fields have been combined – though there are usually traces left behind. There is a well-known example of a route described in a very popular book of walks, which contained an instruction to turn by the cottage with the corrugated iron roof, but the owners thatched it. They eventually became so exasperated with helping out bewildered walkers that they were forced to put up a sign announcing that this was indeed the tin-roofed cottage. In time every walker will find that the compass really is the most trustworthy of all aids.

This has been a general introduction to the most basic notions of how to devise a walk, but one of the great beauties of the British countryside is its infinite variety. Another OS sheet will provide a different landscape with different interests leading to walks of a quite different character. It may contain symbols not present on other maps, such as the crossed swords with a date indicating a battlefield.

Enthusiasts hunt out such sites, but the casual passer-by may see nothing to indicate a spot where blood flowed freely. The Battle of Sedgemoor of 1685 is duly marked on Landranger 182 (ST352355) and to the inexperienced eye there is little to show and the landscape has, not surprisingly, changed a good deal over three centuries. But knowing the events occurred can alert one to the possibilities of finding something of interest in the neighbourhood. Nearby Westonzoyland has a typically beautiful and grand church which boasts a massive studded door with an immense lock, more suitable for a gaol. And a gaol it was for a time, for five hundred men from Monmouth's defeated army were held here after the bat-tle, of whom five died of their wounds and 22 were later hanged.

At other sites, only a little imagination is needed to recreate the scene. Walkers along the ridge at Edgehill in Warwickshire may picture the day in 1642 when Charles I's troops looked down from the heights at the Parliamentarians grouped in the fields below (LR151, SP3549). How easy it must have seemed to charge down and scatter them and win the first conclusive victory of the war. In the end it decided nothing.

In the next few chapters I shall be looking at that diversity to see what underlies it and to try and see how that knowledge can be used to help in planning walks and to make the walks themselves that much more interesting. If a look at one pair of maps has whetted the appetite, do not worry about running out of subjects: there are still another 203 Landrangers left to explore, not to mention over one thousand Pathfinders.

The old military road heading across Rannoch Moor to Glencoe.

Chapter 3

PATHS, TRACKS AND ROADS

It is a cliche, but none the less true for that, that Britain is a crowded island. This means that, in much of the country, walkers are constrained to follow recognised footpaths and rights of way. There are areas, mainly mountainous regions, where it is possible to roam freely unhampered by walls and fences, but even here it is often wisest for those without a detailed knowledge of a region and a good deal of experience to stick to recognised routes. So, once again one is taken back to the map as a starting point. Assuming that no one really wants to walk along a busy road, that still leaves an abundance of choices.

Roads are marked differently on Landranger and Pathfinder maps, though the same general rule applies, that the narrower the road is shown on the map, the narrower it will be on the ground. This, in turn, means that the narrower the road, the less traffic it is likely to carry – though it is always a good idea to assess whether or not it might make a useful short cut for motorists wanting to avoid a town or other obvious obstacle. It is almost impossible in many areas to devise a walk of any length that does not include at least one stretch along minor roads, but that does not mean that such a walk will be lacking in interest. Many country lanes have their own particular charm and individuality. A lane in Devon, for example, may be sunk down between high banks, effectively obliterating all the wider views, but the way might also be brightened with wildflowers on the verge and the insects they attract. Here there is a sense of being almost swallowed up in a cosy, enclosed world. In contrast a road over a northern fell or a Scottish moor will often be totally open and unfenced, with immense panoramas. Wide, grassy margins means there is often no need to even so much as tread on the tarmac.

There is another category of minor road, often known as a 'white road' because it is left uncoloured on the map. This is described, somewhat unhelpfully, in the OS Key to symbols as 'other road, drive or track'. There is absolutely nothing on the map to indicate whether this is a route open to walkers or not, though sometimes there are very strong hints. If a white road leads up from a public road to a private house or farm, then it is almost certainly a private driveway. If it joins clearly defined rights of way, which would otherwise peter out in the middle of nowhere, then there is every chance it can be used as part of a through route. But walkers should be aware that they have no legal right of way along such tracks. If in any doubt, and if an alternative is available, it is generally best to use the alternative. On some maps, particularly the recent Explorer series – drawn to the same scale as Pathfinders but covering a larger area – some of these problems have been eased by including a category of 'permitted path', where landowners are happy for paths and bridleways across their land to be used. Even these, however, carry the warning that such permission can be withdrawn at any time.

There are other restrictions that might be applied, and which will not appear on any map. Perhaps the most important of these relates to taking dogs on walks in the country. The law states that dogs must be kept 'on a lead or under close control' on all rights of way. Sadly some walkers' notion of 'close control' extends no further than ineffectually shouting at a misbehaving animal. There has been a good deal of debate recently on walkers' right of access, but such right also demands that walkers behave responsibly. It is not unknown for dog-owners to state cheerfully that their dog is quite harmless and 'just having fun' as it 'plays' with a flock of sheep. Unfortunately, this is a concept not so easily explained to an harassed ewe. All dogs should be kept on leads when in fields containing livestock, and should never in any circumstances be allowed near sheep. This is especially true in winter and spring when the ewes may be pregnant, and at such times even a dog on a lead can cause anxiety in flocks. The farmer, will, quite rightly, be incensed if he finds the 'playful, harmless' dog's behaviour has resulted in one of his valuable ewes aborting.

In mountain areas where livestock roam more widely this can be every bit as great a problem as it is in a neatly fenced field. In Scotland, where the 'right to roam' is less stringently defined than the 'right of way' in England & Wales, landowners may impose a total ban on dogs at all times or for certain times of the year. This may even apply to well recognised long-distance routes: part of the West Highland Way, for example, is regularly diverted during the lambing season. The problem for the walker who likes to take a dog along is that it is often difficult to find out about restrictions in advance: the safest rule is only to take dogs where you are certain that they are permitted and always make sure that they are appropriately controlled. This may involve avoiding any area with livestock at certain times of year.

Most walkers look out for the routes shown as byways, bridleways and footpaths, and the distinction is important. Byways may run – indeed often do run – over beautiful, open countryside, but they are open to every type of vehicle. A good example of this is the long-distance footpath The Ridgeway, the western part of which runs high over downland in Oxfordshire, Berkshire and Wiltshire. This is an immensely popular route with walkers, but is also growing in popularity with motor cyclists and the ever increasing numbers of off-road motorists, with 4-wheel drive vehicles. The result is inevitably deep rutting, providing an uncomfortably uneven walking surface in dry weather and a quagmire in the wet. There is no doubt that there is a real conflict of interest here between those who want to enjoy the peace of the countryside and the other users, which will surely have to be resolved at some time. In the meanwhile, those who use byways need to be aware of what they might expect, which on one recent walk for the author meant sinking over the boot tops in mud.

Bridleways offer a less drastic problem, and are spared the noise of engines and the stench of fumes, but horses reduced to a narrow path will churn it into brown porridge in no time at all if the weather is bad and the growing number of mountain bikers, who are also free to use bridleways, do nothing to improve matters. That leaves footpaths, especially those which use stiles, kissing gates and other barriers to vehicles and animals, as the happiest alternative. But nothing is perfect: the whole point about going into the country is to experience the natural world, and the natural world is a messy place – and of all the messes the walker is likely to encounter, the bog round a farmyard gate where cattle have waited for a long time is probably the messiest of all, if only because the resulting gooey mess is made up of less appealing ingredients than mere mud. In short, the best planning in the world will not keep walkers from getting muddy and dirty – and there is nothing to be done about it.

Looking at the map and planning a route often involves very little thought about the historical nature of the path itself. Yet that maze of dotted lines zig-zagging and criss-crossing the map is not there by accident. It represents human needs and human decisions, often taken a very long time ago indeed. Knowing and understanding just a little about how the system developed not only helps in planning, but can add a good deal of enjoyment to the walk.

Archaeology has shown that recognised trackways were in use as long ago as 4000 BC. Animals were moved between winter and summer pastures. Thousands must have travelled well-worn routes to the great centres of worship such as Avebury and Stonehenge and there was an immense trade in artefacts such as stone axes – stone tools from the so-called axe factory of Langdale in the Lake District have turned up in huge numbers in, for example, East Anglia. But once one starts to try and identify these routes, the problems begin. Tradition has it that the main prehistoric tracks were upland routes. For example, a track was believed to follow the line of a band of limestone extending from the Bristol Channel to the Humber, and because this stone was laid down in the Jurassic period, some 200 million years ago, it became known as the Jurassic Way. The Icknield Way follows a band of chalk that separates the boggy fenland to the north from the cloying clays to the south. The chalk ridges of the North and South Downs and the route followed by the modern Ridgeway were also supposed to be recognised ancient trackways. It all makes perfectly good, logical sense: the inhabitants of Britain in prehistoric times probably had no more taste for plodding up to their ankles in bogs than we have – but actual evidence is hard to find.

The proliferation of prehistoric sites, such as burial mounds, along these routes has been cited in the past, but this may be no more than a reflection of the fact that the uplands have remained relatively undisturbed, while the lowlands have been ploughed over for centuries. Paradoxically, one of the few areas where hard evidence has appeared, quite literally, is in areas which ancient man might be thought to have found quite inhospitable, the land of swamp and fen. In the low-lying area of the Somerset Levels, which was a swamp and peat bog in Neolithic times, tracks were laid linking 'islands' in the wetlands to the surrounding high ground. The earliest versions consisted of bundles of twigs laid on the ground, and held in place by pegs, but by around 2000 BC more sophisticated walkways of split logs held above ground by stakes were being built. We know this because the peat bogs over which they were built have preserved them, and radio carbon dating has given us the chronology with the oldest 'roads' dating right back to c.3800 BC. None of this has much to do with walking in the Levels today, since they have long since been drained, but it does help us to appreciate that Neolithic Man was by no means a brainless primitive.

If most of the other tracks have to be taken on trust, that does not mean that one cannot walk them without a great deal of pleasure – and many form the lines, or part of the lines, of modern long-distance walks. For even if we cannot always find acceptable scientific evidence of use, we can use our imaginations. And often such routes provide a path into the world of pre-history. Walk up from Avebury (LR173, SU1070) with its immense henge monument to Fyfield Down, and you will find a landscape dotted with sarsen stones, much like those taken down the hill for the stone circle, and a pattern of ancient fields. It is a way of making exciting connections between the present landscape and an almost unimaginably distant past, while enjoying superb walking over open downland. Whether The Ridgeway was a recognisable 'prehistoric' main road scarcely matters.

The evidence for the Icknield Way being a main transport route is probably stronger than for any other ancient track, and it is somehow particularly satisfying to find a continuity of use. One can walk from the edge of Luton to Ickleford on the outskirts of Hitchin (LR166, TL0826 to TL1731) and discover that the Way is still preserved as a broad green path, cutting through more modern field patterns, diving through woodland, but always remaining close to its ancient alignment. A walk along this route will also take you past a great group of tumuli, or burial mounds, on the summit of Galley Hill, to give you a further reminder of great antiquity. The factors that made such routes seem appealing to ancient man make them equally appealing today, and it does not really require a knowledge of archaeology to make such areas popular with walkers. Those who do have a specific interest in the ancient world will always find them especially attractive, but they are not the only walks that can lead us into the distant past – a subject that will be dealt with in more detail in the next chapter.

When one moves up the historical scale to Roman times, conjecture gives way to historical fact. Some of the old roads, such as Ermine Street and Foss Way, have modern roads along their old alignment, with only their famous straightness to distinguish them from other main roads. But throughout England, Wales and southern Scotland, the OS maps are spattered with the legend 'Roman Road'. Sometimes it is attached to minor roads and footpaths: often it is no more than a line of dots indicating the old course. It is possible to make one's own long-distance walks by trying to follow some of these routes. One could, for example, try and follow Akeman Street from Cirencester, Roman *Corinium Dobunnorum,* which still retains its Roman grid pattern of streets and amphitheatre, to the

Roman Akeman Street in Oxfordshire, the aggar still clearly visible as a raised path through the fields of grain.

The Roman road over Blackstone Edge, one of the few to survive with a recognisable surface of stone. Its construction compares very favourably with that of the 18th-century military roads of General Wade.

Roman garrison town of Alchester, close to the modern garrison town of Bicester. It is a walk full of variety, some of it on minor roads, some on cross-country footpaths. There are sections where the Roman road can be seen as a dark streak across a neighbouring field but cannot be walked, and parts where it crops up in most unexpected places, running, for example, as a clear path and right of way right through the parkland of Blenheim Palace. There is even the pleasure of disproving an old cliche, that Roman roads always run straight, for in crossing the River Leach, the road curves down the valley side to ease the gradient (LR163, SP1806). Such a walk can be great fun, combining the familiar pleasures of any walk with the added excitement of historical detective work. But such an exercise is, of course, only possible if one knows what the remains of a Roman road should look like.

The most common method of construction was to build up a good, well-drained embankment or 'aggar' often using material dug out of trenches to either side of the road, which then acted as drains. Stones were laid on the aggar, and topped with gravel . . . Today all that we usually see is the aggar, which remains as a very distinctive landscape feature. There are, however, just a few places where the surface stones are still in place: examples can be seen at Blackpool Bridge in the Forest of Dean (LR162, SO652087) and Blackstone Edge in the Pennines (LR109, SD9817), both of which are in very attractive, if very different, settings. But by far the best example, in terms of both the extent of its preservation and the grandeur of its setting, is to be found high on the North Yorkshire Moors near Goathland, known today as Wade's Causeway. It can be seen at its best near the Wheeldale Lodge youth hostel (LR94, SE8198) and it appears as a prominent aggar, topped by large paving slabs, with beautifully constructed stone culverts for drainage. Seeing such a road, built nearly two thousand years ago, really does bring home the superiority of the technology which did so much to create and hold together the immense Roman Empire. It is so good, in fact, that it seems to have been assumed that it must be a more modern creation and was therefore credited to General Wade, who built up another system of military roads in Scotland and the North of England in the aftermath of the Jacobite Rebellion.

It is interesting to compare the work of the Roman military with that of their eighteenth-century successors, and particularly satisfying that one can do so by moving from the heather moorland of Yorkshire to the Highlands of Scotland. The West Highland Way uses a part of the old military road across

The bridge that gave its name to Bridge of Orchy, built around 1750 by Major Edward Caulfield to carry General Wade's road, and one of the most handsome of all the military bridges.

Wade's road is not merely historically interesting, but passes through some of Scotland's finest scenery.

the wastes of Rannoch Moor and out over the mountains that close in Glencoe. It has to be said that the Roman road appears the better surveyed, and the better engineered of the two – though the military engineers of the later age could claim with a good deal of justification that they had to contend with a far more rugged terrain. This is seen at its most dramatic in the path that zig-zags out of Glencoe, known as the Devil's Staircase (LR41, NN2157) and continues as a scarcely less difficult route to Fort William. Following either route, ancient or modern, is a pleasure, and the walker is likely to be more struck by the similarities of the two roads than their differences. We may have leaped across many centuries, but it is probably fair to say that no road was built in the intervening period of anything like the same quality. So, where does the rest of the complex web of roads, tracks and paths that cover the country fit into the overall pattern of development?

A beautifully constructed culvert on Wade's Causeway

It is convenient to turn back to the distinctions made at the beginning of the chapter – and again main roads will be left out of the discussion. There is a famous line of G. K. Chesterton's: 'The rolling English drunkard made the rolling English road.' It might be more accurate to say the wealthy English landowner made the rolling English road. Time and again one will find minor roads contorted through extravagant angles, not to cope with a difficult terrain, but in order to avoid encroaching on the land of some great estate or important holding. This may be extremely irritating for motorists, but is very much to the benefit of walkers, who enjoy a constantly changing viewpoint. For centuries, local roads were the responsibility of local people, and the importance of different routes varied as settlements either grew or declined. When road improvement became widespread in the eighteenth century, a pattern was set. Some routes were allowed to remain as tracks, while some were given a brand new surface and blossomed into roads. At the same time wholly new routes were built by the turnpike trusts, who charged users for the privilege of travelling in comfort. These too have often suffered changing fortunes. What was once quite the latest thing in transport infrastructure may now be reduced to country lane status or even, on rare cases, a mere track. But they have left behind memories of former glories. When the trusts were given permission to build new roads, they were required by law to provide milestones and signposts, and milestones, in particular, are always of interest. Some are plain, curved stone blocks, others have quite elaborate lettering and it is not uncommon to find cast-iron plates set into the stones. They are intrinsically interesting – and provide a useful check on progress. The other feature of the turnpikes was the toll house where the money was collected. These were generally set at junctions and are often hexagonal in plan, providing the toll collector with a good view along the road. Country roads have many such hints about their own past to keep the walker interested, but most of us still look forward to quitting the tarmac for a walk across country.

An elaborate milestone in Fife. Many such stones were erected along the newly constructed turnpike roads, and are as decorative as they are useful.

Paths and tracks are even more varied in their origins than country roads. The more important tracks, the ones which today are likely to be designated as bridleways, are often distinguished from the surrounding farmland by having quite clearly marked borders, running between fences, hedges or walls. Some may once have had the same status locally as others that have now been dignified by surfacing. Such tracks come in an immense variety. In some cases, centuries of use have worn them down until they have sunk between high banks and the process has only stopped at the bedrock. Some are narrow, some broad; some grass or trodden earth and a few may even be cobbled. They may have served a whole variety of purposes.

Up to and beyond the arrival of the turnpikes and the canals that eased the movement of goods in the eighteenth century, much of the commerce of the country was carried out by strings of pack animals. One distinctive feature of the pack-horse route was the bridge over river and stream. There was no need for wide bridges as the animals, horses or mules, moved in single file, and the spans could be built with high arches to reduce the material needed. Parapets were always low, to allow extra space for the broad packs to pass above them.

The steep arch of this bridge in Glen Livet makes it clear that it was not intended for vehicles, but was meant for pack horses and for pedestrians.

Following these old routes is almost invariably rewarding. They are particularly associated with the textile trade – though by no means exclusively. If one goes to a typical small mill town or village, such as Marsden at the end of the Colne Valley leading out from Huddersfield (LR110, SE0411) one is likely to find a pack-horse bridge somewhere nearby – in this case, close by the church. From here a whole network of paths lead away up the surrounding hills. Even far from the centre, there are cobbled sections, particularly on steep gradients, and there are always discoveries to be made along the way – an old water-mill, once used for spinning yarn perhaps, or the cottages with their typical long row of windows at the upper level, where hand-loom weavers worked.

The other major routes were the drove roads, used to take animals to market or to move them between winter and summer pastures. An immense network of drove roads spreads across Wales, where the cattle were collected and brought to England for fattening and sale, and to Scotland. Sometimes the clue is no more than a lonely moorland inn – and if it happens to be called the Drovers Arms, that helps. Many of these are very definite tracks, and in places have been incorporated into walks, as on a section of the Southern Upland Way, where the old drove road is followed across Minch Moor (LR73, NT3533) to the east of Traquair. This is a high-level route with plenty of reminders of its old use in the shape of sheep folds and shelters and the curious Cheese Well spring where drovers left a morsel of cheese as an offering to ensure a safe journey.

It is impossible to list all the different origins of existing tracks, but each was developed to serve a particular purpose – to provide access to mine or quarry, to move commodities ranging from salt to sheepskins, and it is rare to find no hint of old uses somewhere along the way.

By far the commonest form of footpath makes up a complex network linking farm to village, village to village, village to town. These are the paths that have been used by countless generations moving from their houses to work in the fields, to visit friends and relations, to carry out the everyday business of a community where most people had nothing but their own two legs to move them from place to place. Take almost any map and you can see just such a pattern, established who knows when, accepted by long usage until the paths became formalised as rights of way. However much the use of the surrounding land might change, the way remained until, in England and Wales, the law upheld the right of anyone who chose to walk it and allowed no one to obstruct it. Scotland has a different system. A glance at a Scottish map can be quite dispiriting in that there seem to be very few footpaths marked and even these – as the key makes clear – are not 'rights of way' but paths accepted by general usage. This does not, however, mean that areas are closed. An Access Concordat signed by landowners' associations and interested bodies including the Scottish Ramblers Association allows free access to the hills and a number of other wild areas. This freedom to roam is much cherished, but there may be restraints imposed from time to time. There are two seasons in particular when walkers need to be aware that there may be restrictions on their right to roam, not least for their own safety. Deer stalking takes place between the middle of August and the middle of October, grouse shooting from 12 August to 10 December. Information about these activities can be obtained through the Countryside Ranger Service and local Ranger Service.

On farming land there are the paths that walkers use all the time, without perhaps thinking very much about them. Yet it is an extraordinary thing. Time and again one will find a path that slices right through the middle of a field of corn so that in high summer all one can see of passing walkers are heads and shoulders moving above the grain. This is such an important right, directly affecting everyone who takes country walks, that it needs always to be vigorously defended. At the same time, there are obligations on the walkers to keep their side of the arrangement. Not all paths are signposted: ways are by no means always clear. This is where the Pathfinder maps are invaluable. Because field boundaries are shown, it is at once clear, for example, on which side of a hedge one is supposed to walk. This may seem trivial, but the right of way is very specific – and there might be no right whatsoever to walk on the opposite side. Even if no one objects, there might be no way of getting out at the other end of the 'wrong field', whereas when one is on the right track there will be – or should be – the reassurance of gate or stile. The landowner has an obligation to keep the path clear: the walker has an obligation not to abuse the privilege. As a general rule the system works very well, but there are farmers and landowners who object to anyone crossing their property, even when they have a legal right to do so. It is intimidating to find a stile criss-crossed with barbed wire, a large notice saying 'Dangerous Bull in Field' or even a peremptory 'Keep Out' – not to mention a large farmer with a shotgun. How far an individual is prepared to stand on his or her rights is a matter of personal choice – but even if forced to beat a retreat, it is always worth reporting the matter to the appropriate local authority. Those who deny walkers their right of way are, quite simply, breaking the law.

In general, local councils are responsible for maintaining rights of way, but they do not have the resources to check every single footpath over a vast area of ground. So, it is up to walkers to report these breaches in the law. The principal group to take responsibility for this chore is The Ramblers Association. It is a very good idea not only to contact the council where any illegal blockage is found but also to pass on the information to the Ramblers: they have a much more efficient and powerful system for dealing with any such complaint than an individual walker. At the same time, walkers should use commonsense. Often there is an unwritten

Haytor tramway is perhaps Britain's most unusual railway. Horses pulled trucks along the stone rails, complete with stone points, that served a large granite quarry on Dartmoor.

agreement between a local farmer and walkers that although the legal right of way heads straight through the barley, visitors will cooperate with the farmer by going round the edge of the field. This way everyone is happy and unnecessary conflict is avoided. This does not involve relinquishing rights, and if the farmer then decides to take a bit more, and plough right up to the hedgerows, then the walker is perfectly entitled to reclaim the right to march across the middle. There will, alas, always be those who deplore compromise and see it as weakness: the farmer who wants no one on his 'private' land and the walker who insists on abiding by the letter of the law. The happiest solution, however, is surely one in which the farmer makes a living from the land, rather than selling it off for development, while the walker gets reasonable access to the countryside.

Long-established footpaths and bridleways are not the only tracks that can be walked. In the eighteenth century, engineers began to construct tramways over the main industrial areas, railed tracks along which horses pulled trains of wagons. They have all long since ended their working lives but their remains provide a different and often interesting alternative walkway. Their most distinctive features are the sleeper blocks. The familiar railway sleepers would have been useless as the horse had to walk between the tracks, so rails were mounted on parallel rows of stone blocks. Tramways were particularly popular in the hills and valleys of South

The disused railway is a prominent landscape feature in the Wye valley.

Wales, where they can be found terraced into hillsides. The steep slopes were overcome by inclines – either 'self-acting', where the weight of the full trucks going down was used to raise the empties, or worked by winch, powered by steam engine or water-wheel. One of the many fascinating systems can be found on the Blorenge in South Wales. There is an incline running straight up the hillside from the canal wharf at Llanfoist (LR161, SO285130) and a well marked track encircling the hill, and it can even be followed to the neighbouring hill where it ends in quarries. The oddest variation is the 'granite tramway' running past Haytor on Dartmoor (LR191, SX7577). Because iron was expensive, but stone easily available, the whole system was built using stone rails. They still snake away, complete with stone 'points', across the wide expanses of moorland.

In time the tramway developed into the railway, as the horse gave way to the steam locomotive. Dr Beeching wielded his axe, and 8,000 miles of track were obliterated, disused embankments, cuttings and tracks thread their way across maps. In recent years, it has been appreciated that these are ready-made cycle tracks and footpaths, and more and more have been opened up. Sustrans, formed in 1979 to develop the old Midland line between Bristol and Bath, has now become the major developer of these traffic-free routes. Since then Sustrans has spread their system of paths, often but not always, based on disused railways, to the point where there are now some 1,500 miles (2,400 km) open, with plans to extend the network to 8,000 miles (12,800 km) by 2005.

The appeal to the cyclist is obvious – locomotives do not take kindly to going up steep hills but walkers are often wary about them proving a little dull. Yet they can offer spectacular points of interest. The Waskerley Way is only one of a number of connected railway walks in North East England, and includes a soaring viaduct that stands 150 feet (46 metres) above Hownes Gill (LR88, NZ096490). There are railways in the mountains – the old line through Glen Ogle from Lochearnhead was known as the Khyber Pass of Scottish railways, and anyone walking the line will soon see why. There are seaside lines – one can imagine the days when the Atlantic Coast Express thundered down from Wadebridge to Padstow – and quiet country railways, where the train stopped at every station. In short there is a lot to be said for the old lines, particularly when the more interesting sections are incorporated into longer routes. Walkers do have to be aware that not all the old lines are open for use, and take note of those shown on the map as being rights of way.

Walking paths or tracks always reveals some part of the history of a region, whether it is a prehistoric trackway or an abandoned transport route of the nineteenth century. So each will have its own character, not entirely dependent on the type of landscape through which it passes. This is another factor that helps give walking in the British Isles such immense variety.

The former Caledonian Railway line from Stirling to Oban now provides a spectacular path through the mountains of Glen Ogle – and a reminder of the skills and perseverance of the Victorian railway builders.

A Stone Age house at Skara Brae, Orkney, showing hearth and 'dresser'.

Chapter 4
THE ANCIENT WORLD

The remains of the ancient past are all around us. Some are very obvious – no one is going to overlook Stonehenge, say, or Hadrian's Wall. Others may not be so instantly recognisable. The Ordnance Survey Ancient Britain map shows the location of over a thousand sites, which are referred to as 'major visible antiquities'. They cover an immense timespan from around 3500 BC to the Norman conquest of 1066. As one would expect, they are sparsest in heavily built up areas, which means, conversely, that they are found in precisely the sort of areas likely to appeal to walkers. But these are only the major sites. If one turns to a particular area, the Landranger Map will show a far more detailed picture. Take, for example, map 191, covering Okehampton and North Dartmoor. The Ancient Britain map reveals an impressive selection of twelve major sites. But a look at the Landranger reveals that there are an enormous number of lesser sites, indicated by the use of Gothic script, and certain features crop up all the time – cairn, cist, field system, hut circle, stone row, stone circle, tumuli, settlement and more. In all, there are almost two hundred of them.

If one were to take a walk, which looks from the map to be a sensible thing to do, from Peter Tavy (SX5177) to the Youth Hostel at Bellever (SX6577), a walk of 9 miles (15 km), you would pass White Tor, with cairn and fort, two stone rows and a standing row, more cairns and a cist, a settlement, a homestead and a clapper bridge – there is even an indication of a more modern site in the name of Powder Mills Farm, with a couple of chimneys nearby. It is, however, one thing to see all these names on a map, with sites cropping up at a rate of about one per kilometre, but it is quite a different matter to recognise them on the ground and understand their significance. But it is surely clear that they could well add a great deal of interest to the walk – indeed, for many, having such a proliferation of points of interest could well be a factor in choosing this particular route rather than another. Most of these sites will be easily recognised by trained archaeologists, but might just as easily be overlooked by the rest of us – and even if we do see them we could well be

The entrance to the great walled enclosure of Grimspound on Dartmoor. Inside the ring are the remains of a score of stone huts, home to Bronze Age people around 3000 years ago.

puzzled as to their importance, or where they fit into the overall picture of life on the moor. What one is seeing, in fact, is a small part of a pattern of settlement that covered much of the moor during the Bronze Age. Along this walk, one receives hints of this, but it helps to make sense of these smaller sites if one has first seen the really big, impressive remains to be found on Dartmoor. For example, to get a clearer idea of what the single word 'settlement' might mean, and to give real significance to the numerous 'tumuli' and 'cairns' one could take an alternative walk, from Widecombe in the Moor (SX7176) following a splendid open ridge to Hameldown Tor and Grimspound (SX701809). On Hamel Down, cairns and 'Two Barrows' are marked. In fact, one of the two barrows is the really distinctive feature – an immense circular mound, with the traces of a ditch round it. This is typical of the round barrows, which were used for burials in the Bronze Age. Further along is an even more impressive feature, known as 'Broad Barrow'.

Grimspound is perhaps the most extraordinary ancient site on Dartmoor. It consists of a compound enclosed by a stone wall, as much as 9 feet (3 metres) wide and 3 feet (1 metre) high, which was probably used by a cattle-rearing community. Inside the ring are twenty hut circles. At their simplest, they are small circular buildings, with an entrance, but no roof. Originally, a pole would have been set up on a central stone to form the basis of a conical roof of wood and thatch. There are traces of cooking areas and ledges which may have held bedding. These were the homes of farmers who came here about 3000 years ago. It makes a most memorable climax to a walk.

The interest of ancient history lies partly in the glimpse it gives into everyday life so long ago – but also in the many puzzles it presents. It really takes little imagination to envisage Grimspound as a working cattle farm. We might wonder why such a vast mound had to be created for burials, but we can clearly see that it must have had a spiritual significance for the people of the time. But what of those other names scattered across the map – standing stone, stone circle, stone row? An alternative route from Peter Tavy could have led south toward Princetown, and just beyond Merrivale, the name 'Stone Rows' appears and 'Stone Circle' (SX5574). Here are a single and two double rows of small stones, the largest row stretching for about 285 yards (260 metres) and containing over 200 stones. Nearby is a circle of 11 stones and a single stone, over 9 feet (3 metres) high. There is no shortage of theories about such groupings, which range from the cautiously prosaic, that they have a religious significance that we can no longer ever begin to understand, to the fanciful notion that they were laid out as landing strips for extra terrestrial visits, or were sources of magical

Standing stones on Machrie Moor, Arran. This impressive Bronze Age monument is part of a complex system of stone circles, which are linked in legend to the giant Fingal.

power. Whatever one might think, they are undeniably fascinating, and it would be a pity to spend any time walking on Dartmoor without seeing at least one of these mysterious sites.

What we have done so far is look at just one map in terms of the remains of just one period of prehistory. Other maps would show other patterns, but by no means necessarily less interesting ones. Rather than looking at different regions to see what they have to offer, it is just as well to get some idea of what one might find surviving from the various periods.

In general, the earliest period for which there is any very large number of visible sites is the Neolithic or New Stone Age, which is generally taken as lasting from around 3500 to 1700 BC. The popular image of the Stone Age is of primitive men and women, dressed in animal skins, using lumps of rock tied on to sticks as tools. In reality, they were a good deal more sophisticated than that image suggests, and the more one encounters the surviving physical evidence from that remote time, the more impressed one is by these people. It is worth looking at this period in some detail, simply because it would seem on the face of it that there would be little to see from so long ago. In fact, there is a great deal – which gives an idea at once of just how rich the scattered remains of the periods we call prehistoric and ancient really are. If we start with the stone tools from which the name Stone Age derives, one gets the first intimation of technical skills. One is, of course, far more likely to see stone implements in a museum than one is to pick up a stone axe-blade or flint arrowhead when out walking. But there are a few places which could well be met along a walk that show that those ancient people did more than just pick up any old rock and work with it. One of the commonest materials found all over the chalk downland and other chalk areas is flint. You can pick up lumps of it all over the place, and it is easy to see how the nodules have broken off leaving sharp edges. It is no great imaginative leap from this discovery to realise that, with a little practice, one could hit the flint with a harder stone to create sharp edged flakes that could be fashioned into knives, scrapers and arrowheads, or that the large fragments that remained could be smoothed and polished to make axes. This process, known as knapping, was at the heart of Neolithic man's attempts to tame the wild countryside.

He went further than this, however. He also found that some flints suited the purpose better than others, and that these were often found some way beneath the surface. So he sank pits down, and dug out galleries from the bottom. In short, Neolithic man became a miner. By far the most spectacular site is Grimes Graves in Norfolk (LR144, TL8189). The ground looks like the aftermath of an artilllery bombardment, with hundreds of craters scarring the ground. These are collapsed pits, surrounded by rings of spoil and debris

Those who are fortunate enough to have a chance to explore one of these mines will find a complex of low galleries leading to the wide bands of shiny flint. I well remember the thrill of crawling to the end of a passage and shining a torch through to another gallery which was just as it was when work ended, with a pick axe made out of a deer antler casually propped against the wall. And this is only one of many such sites, and once one has seen it, then recognising others becomes a good deal easier. Yet of the many walkers who tread the South Downs and visit Cissbury Ring – literally one of the high points of the region (LR198, TQ131082) – how many recognise what they are seeing? Most will be aware of the ramparts of the hill fort, but might easily overlook the pock-marked landscape around the western and northern slopes. Flints were not the only stones used, and in other mountainous areas, such as the Langdale Pikes in the Lake District, Penmaenmawr in North Wales and Ben Lawers in the Scottish Highlands, there are hillsides spattered with flakes and partially formed implements from these old open-air axe factories.

If these people's implement-making was more sophisticated than one might have expected, what about their homes? Every cartoonist shows them living in caves, and it is very rare to find actual remains. To see really well preserved examples, one has to travel far north to Orkney or Shetland. Here, where stone is plentiful and wood scarce to non-existent, small houses were built in a far sturdier fashion than the later huts of Grimspound. For those who enjoy walks far from the more crowded, popular areas, these islands really offer something special – and for those who want to plan their walks around prehistoric sites, they are unbeatable. Skara Brae on Orkney (LR6, HY221187) is a Neolithic settlement on the shores of the Bay of Skaill. It is extraordinarily well preserved, thanks to two freak storms: the first inundated the tiny village, covering it in sand and driving out all the inhabitants; the second storm, in the middle of the last century, blew the sand away. It was Britain's Pompeii, with everything preserved, right down to the house furnishings, including what can only be described as a Stone Age dresser. These are recognisably houses with cooking areas, beds and tables, and it is not hard to imagine them as being quite cosy, even in the bleakest winters. But this is only part of the Neolithic story.

From Skara Brae one can walk down by the shore of the Loch of Stenness, and discover two magnificent and beautiful monuments. The Ring of Brodgar a henge, one of that great category of ceremonial sites that includes Stonehenge and Avebury. There is an immense ditch, cut 9 feet (3 metres) down into the bedrock, with an internal bank and two entrances to the 155-yard (142-metre) diameter circle. Inside of that is a ring of stones of which 27 survive, the tallest being nearly 16 feet (5 metres) high. It rivals any of the great stone circles of Britain, not least because of the majestic setting; and that

The well preserved huts of the Neolithic village of Skara Brae.

is not the end of the story. Nearby is a second henge, smaller in diameter, but with immense standing stones. Then, beyond that, is Orkney's greatest glory, the chambered barrow, known as Maes Howe. The immense mound, 38 yards (35 metres) across, covers a stone grave. A stone-lined passage leads to the heart of the mound and a great central chamber, lined with stone blocks beautifully jointed together and roofed over, with alcoves running off on three sides. There is nothing primitive here: this is workmanship of the highest order. What it once contained we cannot know, for the Vikings came and sheltered here, and they scratched their messages in runes on the wall, and proudly announced that they had robbed the tomb of its treasures.

No one can pretend that there are many walks anywhere in Britain that can produce such a wealth of superb sites. Yet there is a huge amount to be seen, and it always seems so much more exciting to walk to such sites, to see them appear first on the horizon, then grow more distinct, than it is to be brought by a coach to queue for a ticket. Many Neolithic sites are to be found in remote, wild country which adds immensely to their appeal. We feel, in imagination at least, closer to the ancient landscape. This is true of Pentre Ifan (LR145, SN099370) a chambered

The chambered long barrow of Pentre Ifan. Today it looks like an eccentric stool for a giant, but what we see is a burial chamber stripped of its protective mound of earth.

Where the Dorset Coastal Path strikes inland north of Weymouth, walkers are confronted by an immense array of vast earthen burial mounds – a Bronze Age cemetery.

long barrow where the protecting mound has long since eroded leaving the stones exposed like some monumental sculpture. It stands in the Preseli Mountains of Wales and one can walk the ridge of these hills and find crags and broken rocks that supplied the blue stones that were carried from here all the way to Wiltshire to become part of the long development of Stonehenge. As at Orkney, it requires very little effort to devise walks that combine scenic beauty with a sense of deep historic reverberations. This happens time and again.

When one moves forward along the chronological scale to the Bronze Age, what is striking is not a sense of violent change, but rather one of continuity. Just to the north west of Avebury (LR173, SU0871) is Windmill Hill, not very high, not very imposing – and not even the site of a windmill. It is a pleasant stroll up, with a view down into the great henge, and there are a number of typical Bronze Age round barrows. What is not nearly so obvious are the three concentric ditches which were filled in with all kinds of material from clay figures to human remains. The outer circle is 395 yards (360 metres) in diameter and cut by causeways – hence the name 'Causeway Camp'. It is an important site, for the excavation here showed occupation going back to around 3000 BC and gave a name to the culture of the age, the Windmill Hill people. It is not the most exciting site in Britain, but it is one that stirs the imagination to find how the special aura that this important site had was carried through to a later age.

Early Christians used sites of ancient mystic significance in an attempt to woo the pagan population to their new religion. Here Knowlton church sits right in the middle of a large henge.

An even more remarkable survival of a sense of spirituality being recognised over thousands of years can be found at Knowlton, where there are three henge circles – and there, right in the centre of the middle ring of those ancient sanctuaries, stand the remains of a medieval church (LR195, SU024102). This is clearly an attempt to woo the followers of an ancient religion into following a new, based on the same holy site.

Burial places had a special significance in the ancient world. The long barrow which was typical of the New Stone Age gave way to the round barrow of the Bronze Age. They come in many forms and sizes. The simplest – the bowl barrow – is just a circular mound, though it may have an outer ditch; the bell barrow has a flat area round the mound, then a ditch and then an outer bank. The more ornate bell barrow was strictly reserved for male burials. The other great, distinctive monuments of the age have already been discussed – standing stones and stone circles. One of the fascinations of the age is the contrast between the comparatively humble houses, such as those of Grimspound, and the imposing majesty of the great ritual structures.

One of the most extraordinary walks that cannot fail to impress with the sheer effort that must have been put into creating these immense funerary mounds is the section of the Dorset coastal path that turns inland to avoid the built-up area around Weymouth. All the way from the White Horse above Osmington (LR194, SY7184) to the Hardy monument (SY6187) the route is lined with barrows, with several in sight all the time. It also provides, as a bonus, a view down to one of the mightiest remnants of the age that was to follow, the Iron Age hill fort of Maiden Castle. The walker who takes a circular route along the ridge of Bronkham Hill from the Hardy monument and down past the aptly named Four Barrow Hill to Maiden Castle and back through Martinstown, not only enjoys a splendid route but also starts to get an idea of the differences between these civilisations. For the Bronze Age people the hills and ridges were places where the dead could be given a prominent last resting place. That this was important is obvious – and becomes even clearer if one visits a museum and sees something of the richness of the grave goods excavated from the barrows. It suggests a well organised society in which continuity not change ruled people's lives.

The complex pattern of banks and ditches that make up the ramparts of South Cadbury Iron Age hill fort can clearly be seen in this aerial view. (*Cambridge University Collection of Air Photographs*)

The Celtic people of the Iron Age world, from the evidence, seem to have been a good deal less at peace with their immediate neighbours. The hill fort is their typical monument. Hills provide obvious, naturally defensible positions, and they could be strengthened by digging ditches and building ramparts round the summit. There are over 2000 in Britain but none grander than Maiden Castle. Yet even here there is a continuity. This isolated hill was an obvious focal point for the area and there was a Neolithic camp here, but most of what we see today dates from around 150-75 BC. The ramparts are vast, the ditches deep and the entrances cunningly contrived to bend and twist to put attackers at the mercy of the defenders.

The defences held, and would have held for longer, but the Iron Age people were defeated by a superior technology. In AD 43 Vespasian's Second Legion attacked the fort. The defenders had collected tens of thousands of stones from Chesil Beach for their sling shots: the Romans had the powerful *ballista*, a sort of mechanised bow that hurled bolts and stones. The outcome was not in doubt. Somehow, it is the notion of a country in a state of permanent unease that comes across when one looks at the most impressive monuments of the age. Everyone, it seems, needed a place to scurry away to in times of danger. Maiden Castle seems to have been something of a rarity, a whole settlement, permanently sheltered by its barricades. Other hill forts were smaller, and were places to retreat to in times of danger.

In Scotland, there are even more dramatic strongholds to be seen, duns, brochs and wheel houses, all of which are variations on the defended homestead. The greatest of all is Mousa Broch on Shetland (LR4, HU457236) an immense tower over 50 feet (15 metres) in diameter and rising to a height of over 40 feet (13 metres). Like all brochs it has double walls, the space between the two being occupied by rooms and galleries with a main living space in the central courtyard. One of the attractions of broch hunting is that it almost always involves a walk into wild and dramatic scenery.

People did not, of course, live in permanent conflict. Many even carried on their old style of life after the Roman invasion. At Tŷ Mawr at the foot of the western slopes of Holyhead Mountain (LR114, SH212820) are a series of low stone hut circles, and oblong huts, which seem to have been used as workshops – there are traces of copper slag. From here one can walk up to the top of the mountain to find the crumbly stone ramparts of a hill fort. Life may have been peaceful at Tŷ Mawr – but one could never be too careful. And the people of the little settlement went on with their lives even after the Romans established their fort down beside what is now the modern harbour of Holyhead. Once again a simple walk, which can be taken just for the superb views over a dramatic coastline, takes you right out of one historical period and into another.

One of the most dramatic sections of Hadrian's Wall at Steel Rigg. The wall itself is well preserved, and the square structure represents the remains of a mile castle.

The Roman world comes to us presenting two very different faces: that of the military conqueror and that of the settler – not so very different in some respects from the situation that existed in the previous age. The best known remains are (apart from the road system looked at in the last chapter) the defensive works. That, however, represents only a part of the story. Even walking along the most famous defence of them all, Hadrian's Wall, one is soon aware of other aspects of Roman life. The wall itself is a mighty affair, especially impressive as it reaches its high point above the shattered rockface of Winshields Crag, where the defences seem to march forward relentlessly, as if heading across a flat plain, not switchbacking over the hills. It is easy to think of a frontier guard in one of the lonely mile-castles having a thoroughly miserable existence, like the one in W. H. Auden's *Roman Wall Blues*.

Over the heather the wet wind blows,
I've lice in my tunic and a cold in my nose.

And then one comes to one of the major forts, such as Chesterholm, now better known as Vindolanda, or the garrison at Housesteads. What one is struck with here is the standard of amenities – the baths, the taverns and shops, the commandant's house with its hypocaust system of central heating and, not least important, proper latrines built over a well constructed sewer. At

Looking out over the watchtower at Hardknott Pass in the Lake District. Overlooking the pass itself, it also served as a guard tower for the highly impressive fortress.

another fort, Chesters, there is even a well preserved regimental bath house. If Auden's soldier did have lice it was probably his own fault. There is nothing in Britiain to match the wall for its insight into Roman military life, and it can best be appreciated by those who take the time to walk the entire route, if only because they will share with the Roman soldier the sense of pleasure at finding civilised comforts at the end of a hard day. But it was not the Wall that produced the harshest environment faced by the occupying troops. Anyone who has walked the Lakeland hills in winter knows how harsh conditions can be – and a wet day in summer can be little better. One of the great walks is out of the Langdale valley, up over Bow Fell and down into Eskdale. And there, guarding Hardknott Pass, is the old fort of *Mediobogdum* (LR89, NY218015) in a wild landscape of moor and crag. It is not just that it is a magnificent site, but it provides a climax to the whole walk.

The Romans came to Britain for more than just the love of conquest: they came for the mineral wealth, everything from lead to gold. The Roman gold mines at Dolaucothi (LR146, 6640) have become something of a tourist attraction, but much of what one can see today is the result of later working, first in medieval times, then in the nineteenth century. To see and appreciate the efforts the Romans put in, one needs to walk. Above the ruins themselves, high on the hillside, are wide indentations, from which what now appears as a sunken path leads away. This path can be traced back for around seven miles (11 km), always staying close to the same contour until it reaches a point high up the River Cothi. What one has been seeing is not a path at all, but an aqueduct taking the river water to the mines. The indentations are a type of reservoir which would be filled, then deliberately breached sending water to cascade down the hill in a great flood, sweeping away vegetation and topsoil. This technique, known as 'hushing', allowed the miners to locate the veins of ore without the effort of hacking away half a mountain. If Hardknott Pass is a fitting tribute to the Romans' military determination to hold what they had won, the aqueduct system is an equally impressive reminder of Roman engineering and mining skill. One can see wealth in Roman villas, but it is at places such as this that one finds where it was created.

When the Romans left, a period known now as The Dark Ages began. Saxons, Angles, Danes and Vikings fought the local Celtic people for possession of the land. The period has left indelible marks on the landscape. Hadrian's Wall has its counterpart in the defensive earthwork built in the 8th century by King Offa to separate his land of Mercia from the Celtic kingdoms to the west. It still runs close to the modern boundary between England and Wales. It also forms the basis for a deservedly popular long-distance walk. Even those who do not want to walk the entire length of Wales can sample it. There are few better centres to start from than Knighton (LR148, SO2872), which lies across the ancient frontier. To both north and south the earthwork is at its most impressive, and passes through a magnificent open landscape of hills above the Teme Valley.

We have perhaps strayed a little way outside an accepted definition of 'ancient history', but walking the dyke one can feel the connection to the old Roman frontiers and back further to the ramparts and ditches of the Iron Age forts. History does not leap from age to age: periods merge in a way that would be imperceptible in the lifetime of a single individual. Even the traumatic events, such as invasions did not necessarily bring immediate, or always negative, changes,. We readily accept that the Romans brought a new civilisation when they settled in Britain, but they were not the only ones who arrived as invaders and remained as settlers. Even the Vikings, despite their fearsome reputation, did not devote all their waking hours to rape and pillage. They farmed and fished, and in the far north of Scotland introduced something very new to the region – the watermill for grinding grain. But where the Roman mill had the familiar vertical wheel turning on a horizontal axle, the Norse 'click mill' had a horizontal wheel set directly in the flow of the stream to turn the grindstones.

Dounby click mill, Orkney. The bed of the dried-up stream can be seen with the mill standing directly over it. The simple structure of stone and turf holds just one pair of grindstones.

One of the greatest pleasures, to the author at least, is finding sites which say something about the everyday life of the people of a far distant past. A little cluster of stone huts on the wild flank of Bodmin Moor is more evocative than any museum exhibit can ever be. There is another pleasure, which is just the opposite – discovering mysteries for which no provable answer has ever been supplied. Walk across Ilkley Moor, for example, and you will find strange carvings on the rocks – whirls and circles, and one like a mixture between a swastika and a dancing amoeba (LR104, SE118476). Who were the people who came up to the Cow and Calf rocks and walked along Rocky Valley and left these enigmatic markings? What do they mean? We simply do not know and that in itself is part of the appeal: we are all free to theorise.

It takes time to learn to recognise the marks and monuments left by our ancestors millennia ago, and most of us will probably still be wondering just which bits of stone are the 'cairn' shown on the map and which an accident of nature. Perhaps it does not matter, but identifying what one sees around one is surely a real part of the pleasure of the countryside, whether it is a bird, a plant or an ancient relic. And while it is difficult to plan a walk that will include a particular rare plant or a sight of a particular bird, it is possible to use the map to devise walks that will include interesting prehistoric sites. And most of those who have done so have found their interest growing with every walk.

Regimented tree-planting at Micheldever, Hampshire created formal rides.

Chapter 5

FIELDS AND WOODS

It is difficult to take a walk in the British countryside without, at some stage or other, crossing a field. And even in the bare stony uplands, if one does not actually come across fields, the chances are that one will be looking down on them. The field is so much a part of the everyday experience of the walker that it tends to be taken for granted, so that interest rarely goes beyond wondering where a gate or stile is located, or debating whether the large-horned animal in the distance is a placid cow or ill-tempered bull. But precisely because fields are met so often, it is very well worth while knowing a little about them – and, as so often happens, the more one knows, the more one discovers what there is to know, and that can only add to the interest of a walk.

What one soon discovers is that there is still an immense variety of enclosures covered by the simple word 'field'. It is not just the obvious broad distinction between arable land, with its variety of different crops, and pasture. Travel around the country and you soon discover that each region has its own traditional method of creating a boundary, from the high bank, perhaps topped by a hedge, of the West Country to the drystone walls of northern Britain; the long straight dykes of the Fens to the neat, layered hedgerows of the Midlands. Sadly, tradition is increasingly being eroded by the modern farmers' preference for ever larger fields, and the labour-saving efficiency of the wire fence, but enough remains to ensure that the field system retains its local identity. It is not just boundaries that vary. Look at any field system shown on a 1:25 000 map and you will find an extraordinary mixture of shapes and sizes. It may seem wholly haphazard, but the patterns reflect both the nature of the land and the history of farming in the region.

Archaeologists have provided convincing evidence that Neolithic man had already started growing crops, and that he scratched away at the surface of the land with primitive ploughs; though even the most eagle-eyed walker is most unlikely to see any of the evidence. But move nearer our own time to the

Bronze Age and Iron Age and things change very noticeably and the remains of these very ancient fields are in just the areas most favoured by walkers. Down in the rich valleys, generations of ploughing have long since buried traces of the very distant past, but in the 'fringe areas', on moorland, the lower slopes of mountains and on rough, poor ground in general the signs remain. These are often known – rather misleadingly in many cases – as 'Celtic fields', generally quite small and defined by low ridges round the perimeter. They can often be found near downland ridges, for example, but are not always easy to identify, even when the legend 'field system' on the map indicates their existence. In other areas, however, the ancient fields have created dramatic landscapes. Walkers along the Cornish coastal path, near Zennor, for example, will find an extraordinary pattern of minute fields and hut circles (LR203, SW4438). Looking at the same area on the 1:25 000 scale reveals about sixty fields in an area of just 500 metres by 300 metres, where round a modern farm you might expect to find no more than half a dozen in a similar area. The map, however, gives only a hint of what the walker will see. The boundary walls are made up of immense granite boulders, topped by smaller stones – all testimony to the immense effort that went into clearing this moorland area for farming. And the resulting solidity has ensured their survival. Such a system, if it does nothing else, serves as a reminder that farming has had a central role in the lives of the people of these islands for literally thousands of years.

Ancient field systems are, however, comparatively rare when looked at in terms of the immense numbers of fields in the country as a whole. Other, later, developments are much more common. The one thing that many of us remember from our school days is that, in medieval times, villages were surrounded by open fields divided into strips. Occasionally, the system has survived. At the southern tip of Portland Bill in Dorset, there are remnants of a system that dates back to Saxon times, where the open fields were divided into over two hundred strips or 'lawns', divided by drystone walls and 'lynchets' – low earth banks. These are particularly visible in early morning or late evening when the low sun throws the divisions into relief. Another example can be found in an area which is very popular with walkers, the Gower peninsula. Here strip fields can be seen in the area between Rhossili and Worms Head (LR159, SS4187). A walk that combines magnificent scenery and a chance to see this system at its best would include a circuit of the little headland and a climb up to the side of Rhossili Down, from where the pattern of strips can be seen laid out at the foot. It is generally true that quite the best way of seeing any interesting field system is by looking down on it – which is why so many books and articles on the subject make great use of aerial photographs.

Wiltshire and Dorset are counties particularly rich in examples of strip lynchets, and there are many examples such as this to be seen along the Wessex Ridgeway walk.

Strips are also preserved in a specialised form where they appear on hill-sides. Here they become narrow terraces, rows of flat ledges known as 'strip lynchets', which can be seen running around the contours of the hill. They are found in many different parts of the country, but some of the most spectacular examples in popular walking country are on the Wiltshire downland, among which some of the finest are those on the folded hills above Mere (LR183, SS8233), where the slopes can have as many as twelve quite distinct terraces.

By far the most common form in which a medieval field system is preserved is as a 'fossilised' landscape. This occurred with a change of use, when old ploughed fields were converted to grassland for grazing. The old system is known as ridge and furrow, and was caused by constantly ploughing a narrow strip. Before the advent of the two-way or 'turnover' plough, the ploughman worked in 'stints' – turning the soil away from two parallel furrows on either side of a strip until he reached the middle. Repeated over centuries, this process left a series of parallel hollows and mounds which we can see today when the field is covered in grass as a vast, green, corrugated sheet – often with more modern field divisions cutting across the old pattern. Finding such a system on a walk is always interesting, if only because it throws up another possibility. When arable land was changed to grazing land, the whole pattern

This aerial photograph of Braunston shows the intricacy of the medieval field system preserved under grass – and the antiquity of the lane snaking through it. *(Cambridge University Collection of Air Photographs)*

of rural life was changed as well. Many hands were needed to till and tend the fields: but one shepherd could look after a large flock. As a result a village might decline, shrink or even be totally abandoned. This was not the only reason that villages became deserted – plagues were another common cause – but the introduction of sheep was particularly important in the English Midlands.

For those who like a little detective work on their walks, the hunt for deserted villages perfectly fits the bill. Sometimes they are named on the map in the Gothic script used for all antiquities: for example, Martinsthorpe Village in Leicestershire (LR141, SK865046). What one finds on the ground is an old footpath system, radiating out from what is now an isolated farm. Around it is a very distinctive pattern of ridge and furrow, but immediately next to it are flat areas and hollows, all that remains of the village and its homes. Other clues may appear in the shape of an isolated church, left behind when the village decayed, or a grand house or manor standing in isolation. But overlying these old field systems there will almost invariably be a more modern one, created by enclosure.

The process of enclosing old areas of common and open fields began in medieval times and gathered momentum after the dissolution of the monasteries, reaching a peak in the great age of agricultural improvement, the eighteenth century. Enclosure involved the creation of fields, closed in by hedges, walls or fences. As a very general rule, the smaller and more irregular the field, the older the enclosure. There is a more reliable method of dating some fields – and that is by dating the hedge along the boundary. There is a simple rule that says that if you count the number of species in a 30-yard (30-metre) section of a well maintained hedge, then the total number of species will correspond to the age in centuries. No one seems certain why the method works, but checking it against known dates confirms that it does indeed work in practice. These are the fields which have created what we now think of as the typical rural scene, a patchwork of neat fields, which in the case of later enclosures can be as regular as the squares of a chessboard. But having said that, there is still a wealth of variety, particularly when moving from one region to another.

Ridge and furrow again, but now surrounding a pattern of house plots. The farm is now all that survives of the medieval village of Martinsthorpe. (*Cambridge University Collection of Air Photographs*)

The first variation comes with availability of material. Just as the prehistoric farmers of Zennor used the stones they cleared from the ground to make their walls, so later farmers, struggling with the same problem, found the same solution. The mountains of the Lake District leave precious little space for agriculture, but anyone walking over the hills and dropping down into the smaller villages will find an intricate web of stone walls spread out below them. Those who come to the region to experience the wildness, well away from the tourist crowds, are likely to find themselves at some time or other exploring the region round Wast Water, with its forbidding screes and the rocky peak of Scafell Pike rising high above its western end. There, in among the hills, is the tiny valley of Wasdale Head (LR89, NY1808). A typical Lakeland valley, it would once have been covered in stones, which have been painstakingly removed and either built into walls, or gathered together and walled in, as if like the sheep, they had to be kept from straying. It is an extreme case of what happens in all such regions. In some areas, one can see an absolutely clear distinction between the pasture inside the walled enclosures and the still stony rough ground outside. This does not necessarily imply laziness on the part of the local farmers, but a sensible adaptation to an uncompromising landscape.

Yockenthwaite in Wharfedale shows a typical pattern of drystone walls dividing up the valley into fields that run up to the scrub on the steep slopes at the edge of the moor.

rystone walls in the Pennines. Walls such as these, with their carefully selected stones and neat apping, do as much as anything to give the region its distinctive character.

Anyone walking the Yorkshire Dales, for example, soon becomes aware of n emerging pattern. Down on the valley floor is a crazy-paving-like pattern of ny fields. Above them are larger fields, and beyond that walls stretch out ght to the tops of the hills and on occasions right over the top to the next alley. This is a country poorly adapted for crops, but good for cattle and bet-:r still for sheep. The latter roam free over the hills, finding their own rough razing while the cattle stay on the lower ground – but all rely on the lush 1eadows of the valley for winter feed. Hence one finds the small fields dotted ith the barns which are so typical of the area.

It is all so typical, indeed, that one can easily overlook the care and skill that as gone into creating this well-loved landscape. Its character derives in good 1easure from the drystone walls themselves: they harmonise with the land, ecause the stones from which they were built come from the land. And these are o haphazard piles of stone heaped up together – they are cunning constructions :signed to last. Once the line has been set, a trench is dug about four feet wide 1d deep enough to reach a firm subsoil. Onto this are laid two rows of good,)lid squareish boulders, with the space between filled with smaller stones. Then hat are, in effect, two walls are built up and again the space in between is care-lly filled. At regular intervals large stones, known as 'throughs' are included to

The effect of the stone wall on the landscape depends on the local stone. Here in Derbyshire the pale limestone that threads the hill creates a very different effect from the sandstone further north.

help bind the whole together. The two walls slope very gently towards each other and are finally topped off with a neat capping. Gaps have to be left for gates, and smaller gaps at the foot of a wall – 'cripple holes' – allow sheep to wander from pasture to pasture. In places, a 'through' might be extended to create the 'stone stile' so familiar to walkers in the area. Different parts of the country have their own variations, determined by the type of stone available. In Cornwall, for example, the local slate is often used to create a herringbone pattern wall, which is as decorative as it is practical. The drystone wall is an essential feature of most hill regions, and should always be respected. Clambering over walls can cause damage in a few seconds that can take hours of hard work to repair.

In lusher lands, the patterns are necessarily very different. Here, too, there are still traditional skills to be seen. Hedges come in many varieties, but one of the most satisfying visually is the layered hedge. Hawthorn is commonly used. In the winter when the sap is down and there are no leaves to get in the way, the hedger sets to work. Scrub is cleared, then the upright stems are bent at an oblique angle, after which a cut is made in the branch – deep enough to allow the branch to stay in place but not too deep so as to cause damage. The plants are in effect made to grow horizontally rather than vertically and send out heir prickly shoots in spring to create a solid barrier. Stakes set along the ength of the hedge keep all in order. Sadly, as all walkers in the countryside know, hedgerows have been lost at a terrifying rate in recent years. The extreme examples are the great prairie-like fields of East Anglia, but in others, he easily maintained fence has replaced the hedge as the boundary. For the armer, the advantage is that he can plant his crops right up to the edge and work his fields with ease. The losses are not so easily costed as the gains: the catastrophic decline in numbers of hedgerow-dwelling animals, insects and birds, the replacement of natural beauty with one of man's ugliest creations, barbed wire. It can only be hoped that the proposed new legislation will not ust halt the decline, but reverse the trend altogether.

It is not just the shape and boundaries of fields that have changed: what is grown has altered over time as well. A grass field may seem to be just that – a field of grass with perhaps a faint speckling of flowers. But there is all the difference in the world between an ancient meadow which has never been ploughed for generations and a 'ley', a field sown with one or more species of grass or other fodder crop, treated with pesticides and nitrogenous fertiliser, and probably ploughed up and reseeded every few years. Arthur Young, an indefatigable proponent of agricultural improvements some two centuries ago, described the plants he found in two Oxfordshire meadows in 1813. He listed even different grasses and eighteen other species, ranging from clovers to the delicate bird's-foot trefoil: lucky the walker who finds such abundance today, and what a joy when it does appear.

Crops too have changed over the centuries. In recent years the most dramatic change has come with the dazzling yellow of fields of oilseed rape in flower; and, even more recently, EU subsidies have led to the widespread cultivation of linseed, carpeting the landscape with vivid patches of blue in the late spring. Simply because the effect is so startling it can seem that rape, in particular, is taking over the countryside, but in reality it still represents only a small part of the overall pattern of crops. In southern Britain, wheat still predominates with barley some way behind in second place, though in Scotland barley and oats take the honours. The pattern is distorted regionally, with East Anglia in particular devoting large areas to root crops, notably sugar beet and potatoes. Whatever the crop, walkers must remember that it represents someone's livelihood and be very sure of keeping to rights of way. Not infrequently, local walkers have unofficially rerouted a path to go round rather than across a field. In these cases, it is usually better to ignore the official line and follow local usage, but only when it is a very clear alternative. It may even, in some instances, have been waymarked by the local authority, in which case there is no doubt at all about what to do.

The deer park began as a hunting ground for Norman lords, but by the 18th century the park had become ornamental and the deer were there to be admired not chased. This is Stock Gaylard Park.

An attractive variation on the field is the ornamental parkland, which first came into vogue at the end of the seventeenth century and reached its apotheosis in the work of such designers as Humphrey Repton and 'Capability' Brown in the eighteenth. The image that comes to mind is of undulating grassland, studded with grand trees that made a show, such as oak and horse chestnut, often with a lake, natural or man-made, and ornaments ranging from simple statues to complex follies. Although created to please some great landowner, it is surprising how often there are rights of way across them. Taking just one sheet, Landranger 164, covering an area north of Oxford, there are over a dozen areas of grey stippled patches denoting parkland – and of these over half have rights of way – including the grandest of them all, Blenheim Park. These parks were planted to delight the eye, and still do, so that it makes a good deal of sense to include parkland in any walk where it fits the route.

Originally parkland was very different, having its origins in the deer park and that meant woodland, and woodland is about as likely to feature in a country walk as is a stroll through fields and meadows. The woods we see today appear at first glance to be divided into three categories. First are the large modern plantations of conifer, mainly spruce; second are the large woods and forests of mainly broad-leaved trees or native species and third the smaller woodland patches that dot so much of the landscape.

As one would expect the history of woodland is as complex as any other aspect of the landscape story. Almost all the truly wild woodland has long gone, devoured in a process that began when men first learned to wield a stone axe to clear the land for settlement and agriculture. It is still possible to get some notion of how things must have been from looking at a map such as Landranger 188, covering the Weald of Kent. The southern part of the sheet in particular is predominantly green, and it is not difficult to imagine how little enclosures or 'assarts' were once carved out of the forest, which became ever larger clearings, some just holding one or two farms with fields creeping up to the woodland edge, others developing into villages and towns. A closer look shows, however, that the pattern is not that simple. Every variety of woodland is shown: woods of native deciduous trees, conifer plantations, mixed woods and that very specialised and sophisticated form of woodland, the orchard. One thing, however, is very clear: no walker in the area is going to avoid woodland altogether and even quite small woods present special problems.

The first and most obvious problem is that once you are in a wood, you are very unlikely to find any landmarks to guide you out to the other side. Hereworth Woods, between Maidstone and Sevenoaks is a very large feature, with rights of way running for many miles. It is a complex wood, with blocks of conifer, patches of broad-leaved trees, mixtures of the two, and orchards

It is not difficult to see why this wooded hill at Selborne provided Gilbert White with his favourite view.

huddling all around the edge. Most walkers prefer the more open areas of the broad-leaved wood, with its often rich undergrowth of flowers and ferns to the sterile, densely packed modern plantations, but keeping in the one and out of the other would involve some complicated route planning. It looks quite diffi cult on the map, but will, without any doubt, prove even more so on the ground. The map shows a maze of footpaths and forest tracks.

The easiest plan would certainly be to follow the Wealdway footpath, which is waymarked, but the more adventurous might well wish to choose their own route in which case the problem will then be faced of matching the paths on the map with those on the ground. In woodland, there are few of the constraints found in open country and less need to keep to the track to find a gate or stile. As a result people tend to wander and where some wander others may follow, creating 'unof ficial' paths, indistinguishable from genuine rights of way. Forest managers often put in new tracks when they need to work extensively on one particular area for time. As a result one can easily find oneself on a path which the map shows a heading straight and true with no junctions and diversions, which turns out to pre sent choices every few hundred metres. All one can see in any direction is trees there are no signposts or waymarks, and one path looks as good as another. In these cases there is only one true guide: the compass. Even when the way seems obvious, it is always as well to make periodic checks. We have all at some time gone blithely on along an apparently well defined path, only to find that the route w

ak has been the dominant tree of the Forest of Dean since huge areas were first planted to provide mber for the navy.

anted turned off some way back as a scarcely distinguishable path threading hrough the trees. And even if one selects the right path every time, one can still be iled by finding it closed for logging operations. The walker who can invariably nd the true path through a forest is unlikely to get lost anywhere else.

Having said that often all one can see is trees might make a forest walk seem ull. This is emphatically not so. Different areas suit different trees and have their wn special identities. The steep escarpments of the Cotswolds, Chilterns and owns are home to spectacular beech wood hangers. The trees themselves are hajestic, and when a sudden break produces a view out over the valley the result un be both astonishing and beautiful. At Selborne in Hampshire (LR186, U7433) a specially constructed zig-zag path leads up to a viewpoint made mous by the great amateur naturalist who was vicar here two centuries ago, ilbert White. It is easy to see how he fell in love with such a spot and time has ot reduced its charm nor its grandeur. The experience is very different from that f other areas. Strid Woods near Bolton Abbey in Wharfedale (LR104, SE0656) ke their name from the point where the river is funnelled between rocks to rush own in a narrow gorge. All around are the woods of sessile oak, old woods here the trees crowd in and the walker often has to pick a way through a maze f roots, worn and polished by generations of passers by. And this again is differ-t from a great forest such as Dean where the English oaks rise from their mas-ve trunks to spread their branches wide, creating their own space.

Coppicing was once common, but it is rare now to find a coppice such as this being managed and in use. There has been a small revival in crafts such as the making of hazel hurdles.

The woods offer seemingly infinite variety, and immense seasonal differences, from spring when there may be a carpeting of bluebells to the richness of autumn colours and the bare, stark outlines of winter. What all woodland has in common is the intervention of man at some stage of its history.

Woods were a vital resource for many centuries. In medieval times, there were vast areas of forest reserved for the royal hunts – though the name 'forest' then embraced a whole area, whether wooded or not. Many such areas were carefully demarcated by high earthen banks, up to six feet (two metres) high in some cases, with adjoining ditches. They kept the deer in the deer parks and out of other areas where they would damage the young trees. Often the names 'park' and 'pale' on the map give the clue of what to look out for. Slindon Wood on the edge of the South Downs (LR197, SO9507) is a delightful spot with very grand oak and beech, but it is the name Park Pale that suggests a grand old age, and there, sure enough, you will see an immense bank and ditch.

In later times woodlands were chiefly valued for the wood they produced, which could be anything from 'poles' for making charcoal to timber for construction. In the eighteenth century the Navy was a famous user of timber. A ship was estimated in terms of 'loads' – a vague measure defined as the amount one horse could pull in a cart – and a 64-gun ship used a staggering 2000 loads. But even a modest timber-framed farmhouse used prodigious quantities, perhaps as many as 300 oak and 30 elm trees. Woodland was a valuable resource which needed to be carefully managed. One method was coppicing the underwood trees. They would be allowed to grow for a few years and were then cut back, and new shoots developed from the base or stool. It is less commonly practised these days, but there is ample evidence in many woods, where the stout stools and spindly poles are easily recognised. These were interspersed with the 'standards', the great trees allowed to mature to provide sturdy timbers. Many of these woods have been left to grow wild and form a dark tangle which can have its own romantic appeal. There is something about a dark wood, where trees seem to clutch mossy boulders in roots like talons that seems always to bring back memories of the more terrifying children's fairy tales.

It is not just extensive blocks of woodland that feature on country walks. Many an area is dotted with small patches, which look as if they have been left behind by accident. Often they are coverts, deliberately left for animals and birds, though hardly for their conservation. In Leicestershire there are hundreds of these patches which provide a home for foxes who in turn will provide the quarry for the local hunts. In some cases one will find patches of uncleared woodland on the hillsides above valleys, or small plantations of the evergreen holm oak. These provide a breeding ground for pheasants, which when beaten out of cover fly high above the waiting guns.

Woodland has immense charm and character: in a recent summer walk in the Savernake Forest in Wiltshire, the air seemed full of a great variety of butterflies, a blackcap gave short bursts of richly melodic song and a distant woodpecker provided a rhythmical rat-a-tat accompaniment. Even the dense conifers have their pleasures, with the scent of pine and the sounds of birds heard but seldom seen. And what a delight to walk through Scottish woodland and renew acquaintance with the red squirrel. More than any other type of walk, the woodland walk displays the changes of the year. And there is a history to be read, even if it takes a little effort to reach an understanding.

The chalk cliffs of Dorset, near Lulworth.

Chapter 6

COASTLINE

The popularity of coastal walks is as easy to understand as the popularity of seaside holidays: so many elements come together to create enjoyment. There is the sea itself, whose mood can change so dramatically, from a silky stillness to the roar and crash of waves exploding against a cliff face. Sea birds are a constant delight. You do not have to be able to tell a guillemot from a kittiwake to appreciate their beauty or admire their skill, whether it is the seemingly effortless glide of a gull riding a thermal above the cliffs or the spectacular dive of the gannet as it folds back its wings and hurtles into the sea at a speed of as much as 100 km per hour, to emerge a moment later with its fish dinner. There is the immense variety of scenery – from high cliffs to dunes, miles of flat sand or pebble beaches, salt marshes and reedy estuaries. There is also the comforting thought that this is one type of walk where it is difficult to get lost, at least as long as the sea remains in view. This popularity is reflected in the great extent of official long-distance coastal paths, over a thousand miles of them, headed by the South West Coast Path which extends from Minehead on the Somerset coast right round Land's End to Poole Harbour in Dorset. Other routes are widespread, from the mighty cliffs of Pembrokeshire to the low-lying Suffolk Coast path. One can opt for the gentle walks of the Saxon Shore Way around the coast of Kent or for the – literally – high drama of the Cleveland Way on the coast of North Yorkshire. But even these long-distance paths cover only a small fraction of the available coastline. There are parts of the coast so remote, yet so amazingly beautiful, that one hesitates before even mentioning them. One memorable walk across four miles of desolate, open peat bog at the far north-west tip of Scotland ended at the huge expanse of white sand and gentle rollers of Sandwood Bay (LR9, NC2264) with a tall rock pinnacle standing sentinel over one end. My wife and I had the whole bay to ourselves, with the exception of one curious seal who kept bobbing up from the water to peer at the intruders.

There is one problem very specific to coastal walks: they are necessarily linear. One can walk over and round a hill to create a circuit, but the coast simply goes on and on for thousands of miles until the ring is complete. There is, of course, always the possibility of walking round a small island – a gentle day's saunter round the whole of Lundy, for example, with its high cliffs, rich bird life and

Those who brave the steep climb and precipitous descents of the Dorset Coastal Path are rewarded with views of spectacular cliff scenery, and remarkable features such as the natural arch of Durdle Door.

basking seals is an absolute joy – but, in general, the walker has to make a choice. Will a day's walk be linear, either a there and back route or making use of some form of transport to return to the start, or will it be circular involving a long excursion inland? There is a great deal to be said in favour of the linear walk where it is possible, as there are many areas where the coastline is dramatic, but the hinterland comes as something of an anti-climax. In many ways, planning a linear walk appears to be simplicity itself, as there are immense stretches of coast where paths stay close to the sea edge, but walkers need to think quite carefully about the special difficulties that go with coastal walking.

The most popular areas tend to be those with high cliffs, such as the eastern end of the South West Peninsula walk, from the Isle of Purbeck round toward Weymouth. The map shows all sorts of attractions along the way, including the famous beauty spots of Lulworth Cove and Durdle Door. Landranger 194 suggests a good short walk that stays very close to the sea's edge from Lulworth to Osmington Mills, a modest 6 miles (10 km) – it looks at first glance as if you ould start after breakfast and with a very brisk walk be all the way back again by unch. But look closer at the contours met along the way, and a very different picture emerges. This is typical chalk cliff country, eroded by the sea and the weather, cut deep by small streams to create a mammoth seaside rollercoaster. Up from Lulworth Cove, the path goes to a height of over 300 feet (100 metres), then down it goes again to pass above the natural rock arch of Durdle Door – up down, up down all the way. There are stiff climbs up, and knee-jarring descents on the other side – with the added problem, in wet weather, that ain can transform the chalky paths into greasy nightmares, offering all the adhesion of a bob-sleigh course. Cliff walking can be as tiring as any walk in the mountains. It is tempting to circumvent some of the more severe rises and falls on such walks, and often it is possible to cut round the bottom of cliffs at low tide. On the Pembrokeshire Coast Path, for example, there is a splendid walk from Broad Haven (LR157, SM8613) round the foot of the cliffs from the popular wide, sandy beach to the quiet, narrow harbour of Little Haven, which is offered as an official alternative to the high-level route. But when making such short cuts it is absolutely essential to know where the highwater mark is, shown on OS maps as a continuous black line. In this case, the tide comes right up to

Getting away from it all. There is no road access to Sandwood Bay in the north-west corner of Scotland, ust a lonely path across peaty moorland.

the base of the cliffs. It is vital to know tide times and to be quite certain tha there is enough time for the trip – and that means allowing extra time for slow walking in soft sand. The walker who stays close to the sea's edge needs, like the sailor, to be constantly aware of tide and weather. A gentle lapping of wave: round rocks on a fine still day can turn into waves that have a deadly double action – hurling themselves forward with great force, and sucking and pulling a they retreat. Even more potentially dangerous are wide areas of salt marsh, flat a: can be but cut with an intricate network of streams and creeks. As the tide come: in, these fill rapidly and the tide may advance at an alarming rate.

The circular walk can be a real alternative to the linear. The most successfu are those which make use of genuinely attractive inland features. Many of the islands off Scotland's west coast offer the possibility of a walk along the coast which can be full of interest, combined with a climb into the hills, which is jus as pleasing, but which has the added appeal that as you climb an ever wide coastal prospect comes into view. On one such walk on Arran, there was an unexpected bonus, when a golden eagle appeared suddenly over the brow o the hill and soared up high above the glen. One cannot expect such good for tune, nor even plan for it – only create the circumstances in which it is mos likely to occur. Elsewhere, there may be no hills at all, and not infrequently busy coastal main road provides an unpleasant barrier between the coast an open country. There are few places, however, where a little ingenuity cannot b used to combine the different elements to make a pleasant and interesting walk

High drama at Marwick Head, Orkney. The cliffs are home to immense colonies of noisy, squabbling guillemots and kittiwakes. The distant monument records the sinking of the cruiser *Hampshire* in 1916.

The estuary at Walberswick offers a splendid muddle of improvised buildings, from home-made jetties to tiny fishermen's huts. More solid piers protect the harbour entrance.

For many, the sea is the only element needed to make a walk enjoyable, but the nature of the experience changes very dramatically as one moves from one area to another. In contrast to the high cliffs already discussed, the low, flat coastline of much of south east and eastern England might seem dull, yet this is an area full of interest. When looking at changes in the landscape, one usually thinks of the physical changes brought about by natural forces acting so slowly as to fall entirely outside the scope of human history, while man-made changes work to a much more rapid time scale. This is very far from being the case on the east coast of England. The sea constantly nibbles at one stretch of land only to deposit it somewhere else. The results can be sudden and dramatic: in 1993 Holbeck Hall Hotel in Scarborough was boasting of its fine sea view from its cliff top site. Then the steady erosion of the sea caused a sudden collapse and land slip, and a large part of the building went from cliff top to cliff bottom. Even if events do not move as rapidly as this, there is a steady, slow continuous movement along this coast as sea and land interact.

Southwold (LR156, TM5076) is as good a place as any as a base for investigating this fascinating stretch of coast, not least because it is also one of the most attractive towns in the whole region. It has its own story to tell. Beach huts huddle under the long sea wall, while the beach stretches away into the distance, with its procession of groynes thrusting out into the North Sea to break the power of the waves and stop erosion. As a seaside town Southwold is pure delight, but there is also a majestic church, where painted angels stare down from the roof, peering over an elaborate screen to equally exotic animals carved in the choir stalls. Everything about it shouts wealth, and hints that Southwold once looked to the sea for trade not just for summer visitors. The view is reinforced by the only building to challenge the church for size, the lighthouse that pops up rather surprisingly over cottage rooftops. Here, all the signs point to permanence and stability. But walk down the coast to the River Blyth and a different picture begins to emerge. The river reaches the sea between protective piers, creating a comfortable anchorage for fishing boats and yachts, but the little village of Walberswick which one would expect to find dominating the scene is well inland. Something has clearly changed, and what has changed is the coast itself: the sands and shingle have moved and the old port is a port no more. Follow the river inland and you come to a vast expanse of reeds and marsh before arriving at the village of Blythburgh. Here, too is a church of a magnificence to rival Southwold's, and this too was, in its time, a port. But boats became bigger, too large for the winding Blyth, and left to its own devices the river silted and spread, creating the marshes, lonely places where the marsh harrier can be seen out on the hunt. And if this walk is continued on down the coast, through the wild marshes, one arrives at perhaps the most remarkable site of all, the village of Dunwich. There is no ancient church here to speak of former glories: it crashed to the beach in 1920, taking most of the graveyard with it – and now a solitary memorial stone teeters on the edge. Far out under the waves are Roman Dunwich, Saxon Dunwich, and Medieval Dunwich – all victims of the sea's inexorable progress.

Not content with eating away one part of the coast, the waves in time took the sands and pebbles and plonked them down somewhere else. Further south along the coast is Orford (LR169, TM4249). No need to look very hard for evidence of former importance here, for overshadowing the village is a tall, multi-faceted tower, all that remains of a mighty fortress built by Henry II at the end of the twelfth century. Walk down the main street, however, and the first thought might be that it is unusually wide, and the second that there are some odd indentations. What one is, in fact, seeing is the medieval harbour, now literally high and dry. Continue on down to the sea and the reason becomes clear, for the walk ends not at the sea but at the River Ore, beyond which is a vast sandbank and marsh, Orford Ness, diverting the river to an outflow half a dozen miles further down the coast.

Much of the attraction of coastal walking comes from witnessing this constant battle between sea and land. Along Suffolk's swampy eastern edge it has had striking effects, but there are equally dramatic examples along many of the sea cliffs, where the sea has eaten into the rock to create caves and natural arches, or worn through altogether to create giant rock stacks, such as the Elegug stacks, the romantically named Green Bridge of Wales off the Pembrokeshire coast, or the famous Old Man of Hoy. Man, too, has had his part to play in the shaping of the coast. He has attempted to stem the process of erosion by building ever more elaborate sea defences, and he has searched out every possible natural shelter and then improved it to create ports and harbours. The little fishing port has a unique appeal, with its snug harbour and often close-packed houses. Such places develop because there is a natural gap in the coast to provide protection, and where the gap is small, the houses must fit round it as best they can, often clambering up some steep narrow valley. We think of places such as Clovelly, with its incredibly steep cobbled streets, or Staithes, stuck into a gap in the cliffs, as being beautiful and picturesque, but they are no more than a practical answer to a particular need. The best of them provide natural focal points for walks, especially out of season when the summer visitors have gone.

Sea erosion at Elegug. To the left waves have created a cave; an earlier cave has worn through the cliffs to leave the arch, and a second arch has collapsed leaving the isolated stack.

At Boscastle (LR190, SX0990), for example, a narrow inlet provides what appears to the layman to be an impossible narrow entry made all the more imposing by a blow hole where the waters rush and roar. At the end is a little harbour, with a tiny protective quay. From here one can walk out above the tall Beeny Cliffs, then double back inland to return along the beautiful, wooded Valency valley. It all makes for a delightful walk and villages do not come very much more picturesque than Boscastle. But it is always worth looking beyond the merely scenic to see why such a seemingly impossible harbour was ever created in the first place. The answer is obvious when one looks out from Beeny Cliff and sees just how inhospitable this coastline is when seen, not with the eye of the walker, but that of a sailor. Any haven that could be put to use was put to use. All round the British coast there are small harbours, scarcely used, almost forgotten.

The snug little harbour of Crail.

One of the less used but very attractive coastal paths goes around the ancient Scottish kingdom of Fife. Once huge fleets of herring drifters set out from here, and now just a few remain. But what wonderful places these harbours are. At Crail (LR59, NO6107) a breach in the cliffs gave, once again, just enough space to fit in a small harbour, this time created by two quays, angled towards each other, with a narrow entrance for boats. Harbours come, it seems, in an almost infinite variety, even if the appeal remains the same – weathered stone bollards worn and grooved by countless mooring lines, the play of water and the dancing reflections on the hulls of boats – and all this provided not to please the eye, but as part of the world of one of the hardest, most demanding occupations in the world, that of the fisherman. Not all harbours are fishing harbours, but the essential elements remain the same.

Much of what one sees on a coastal walk looks outwards confronting the age old hostility of the sea – lighthouses, navigation lights, coastguard look-outs are all reminders of the hazards of life on the water. But there are other dangers besides these: the dangers faced by an island race fearing invasion. Amongst the disused fortifications likely to be met are the promontory forts. These are the coastal variations of the more familiar hill forts. The idea is much the same. Use the natural defences supplied by sea cliffs and close off the narrow neck of land with ditch and rampart.

A particularly good example can be found in excellent coast walking country at St David's Head (LR157 SM7227) where the main defensive work consists of a massive drystone wall. Similar ideas were used by the builders of medieval castles. Walking to a castle is a very different experience from driving up, buying a ticket and wandering round for a while before driving off. It gives it a context.

A walk which is almost a seaside history in miniature starts at Beadnell on the Northumbrian coast (LR75, NU2329). The coast road approach is all about the modern seaside, holiday villas, hotels and caravans, bucket and spade and a dip in the briny. But keep going to the very end where the road meets the sea, and a little cluster of rocks provides just sufficient shelter from the waves that cream in across the sands and dash over the rock ledges for the creation of a tiny harbour. And there are mighty reminders that this was a place of some importance long before seaside holidays were even considered. Standing like medieval bastions is a group of eighteenth-century lime kilns. Here limestone was burned, and the lime sent away down the coast, a very important trade: today they provide a handy shelter for lobster pots. A footpath leads south around the great two-mile (3.5 km) sweep of bay with its backing of sand dunes, a delight for holidaymakers, but of no interest to those who look to the sea for a livelihood. It is only when the essential cover of rocky headlands appears, forming the natural protection of Newton Haven, that one finds a tiny fishing village, Low Newton-by-the-Sea. Today everything seems to speak of the sort of modern preoccupations shared by walkers. Splendid scenery, and a concern for the preservation of the local wildlife: Newton Pool is a nature reserve with breeding birds whose populations range from the remarkable sedge warbler, which migrates in winter all the way to Southern Africa, often in a single flight, to the colourful pochards which are generally arriving as the warblers leave. Then comes another great sweep of sand and dunes at Embleton Bay, ended by the highest, rockiest headland along the whole stretch of coast, and it is here that the medieval lords built their great castle of Dunstanburgh. It was begun in 1313 by Thomas, Earl of Lancaster and extended by one of the most famous Lancastrians of them all, John of Gaunt. It is magnificent even in ruins, and its great keep remains a forbidding feature in the land. From the castle the walk can be continued on to yet another small harbour, Craster, where thoughts of war give way to pleasanter notions, as smoke drifts aromatically from the kippering sheds. Three harbours in one short walk speak of a vulnerable coast, where invasion and war were common threats, so the castle has its place and its meaning.

Most of us need no prompting to take a walk by the sea, but a walk such as this shows just how much of interest there is on offer – scenery, wildlife and a fascinating historical context. These are the elements touched on at the beginning of this chapter, which appear time and time again, uniting to give coastal walks their very special character and very special appeal.

The massive weir across the Avon at Claverton.

Chapter 7

WATERWAYS AND WETLANDS

Like the sea, the fascination we find in rivers lies, in good measure, in their ever-changing character. A favourite walk follows the infant River Wharfe up Langstrothdale but its nature changes dramatically with the weather and the seasons. After a rainy spell, the river is a dashing, turbulent affair, rushing and gurgling over a series of rapids; in dry weather, the whole river bed is exposed as a series of flat rock ledges, like a gentle staircase over which a desultory stream trickles down. This is also an area which demonstrates how well and easily such places can be made to yield quite superb walks. We live in an age where water is largely taken for granted: we turn on a tap and expect it to flow to fill a bath tub as readily as a drinking glass. Yet this is really a very modern phenomenon, and for previous generations, river water was a vital part of their lives. A seventeenth-century Speaker of the House of Commons described rivers as 'like Veins in the Natural Body, which convey the Blood into all the Parts, whereby the whole is nourished and made useful'. The narrow green valley, watered by the busy river, was the obvious place to site settlements. So here one finds Hubberholme (LR98, SO9278) with its delightful little church, plain and sturdy on the outside, astonishingly beautiful inside with its carved rood loft and screen, and the old vicarage, now a homely inn with stone-flagged floor. Further up are the hamlets of Yockenthwaite and Deepdale, a cluster of farms built of local stone and wholly at home in the landscape. To walk by the river is a delight, but it can be seen in a wider context by climbing up the hill to the north of Yockenthwaite to emerge at the rim where the limestone is exposed, fissured and cracked to form a natural pavement. Down below the river sits in its deep, scooped-out valley, fed by the hill streams, which are also apt to disappear down pot holes to join the underground water system that has carved its way through the limestone.

Many successful walks can be created in this way, particularly in the upper reaches of rivers, by combining waterside paths with a circuit taking in the hills above the valley. The riverside section described above forms part of the Dales

Way long-distance path down Wharfedale, which in the lower reaches does include a high-level section along the route between Hubberholme and Grassington. Another very attractive long-distance walk that combines walks beside the water with high-level routes down the valley follows the length of the Wye down to its junction with the Severn.

The alternation of hill sections with riverbank walks on the Wye is not entirely due to the wish of the planners to introduce variety. There are many places where the riverside walk is impossible, either because of the terrain or the lack of rights of way. There are also sections where the prospect is unattractive; where, for example, the river indulges in great wayward meanders across the wide Herefordshire plain. It is true of almost every river that the walker will sometimes be forced to turn away to find an alternative route. There may be sections where the river has cut a deep impenetrable gorge through the rocks or, in complete contrast, where it has spread out in low-lying land to create bogs and marshes. The simple statement of intent to walk the length of some particular river may well turn out to be impossible in practice.

Failing to take note of paths marked on a map in genuinely wild and open country is not, in itself, necessarily a bad thing – but can lead to problems. There is a very pleasant walk through Pennant in North Wales (LR135, SN8787), up the valley of the Twymyn. The higher up one goes, the more active the river becomes and the more closely the hillsides crowd in. As the gap narrows, the map shows two paths, one on each side, leading out onto the surrounding hills. It seemed, however, to the author and a friend that it should be possible to stay with the waters to the end. The going became increasingly difficult but – when does it not! – looked better on the opposite bank. We paddled across through the icy cold water and found, inevitably, that things got no better. In the end it was a question of admitting defeat – which would have been the wiser course – or scrambling up a very steep scree slope to the rim of the valley. There was no harm done and no danger, but it could hardly be classed a one hundred per cent success as a walk. Those who stray from recognised paths particularly in tight river valleys should be aware that they may be faced with real difficulties and problems, and should follow the author's advice and turn back if things get impossible – rather than follow his lamentable example.

These are walks that go with the grain of the country, the river providing a natural route to follow. Travel across the grain, however, and the river suddenly becomes a barrier that can only be crossed at a few well defined points, and such places very often become the focal points of settlements. Not the least fascinating aspect of riverside walking is discovering the rich variety of river crossings, from the simple clapper bridge, consisting of flat stone slabs laid over boulders, to the modern road bridge. Follow a river from source to sea, and you will find

The Wye valley has been visited for its beautiful scenery since it was popularised by the travel writers of the 18th century. Here, the Wye Valley Walk winds through the woods near Goodrich.

an immense variety of such crossings, and as great a variety of scenery. One could choose a great river, and walk the newly created long-distance path that follows the Thames from its source in the Cotswolds to the tideway in London. But in this case I would like to look at one of the middle rank of rivers, the Tees, partly because its upper reaches are supremely wild and beautiful and partly because it changes character so dramatically along its path to the coast.

The Tees has its origins in one of the wildest and most remote parts of the Pennines, Cross Fell (LR91, NY6834). This typical moorland fell, its summit plateau ringed by scree like a grubby collar, has its flanks laced by a complex of streams and gulleys. Some drain away to the north, gradually collecting together until finally deciding to head east to join the Tyne; those to the west group themselves as the Eden and head for the Solway Firth, while those to the east and south form the Tees. It is a lonely and bleak birthplace that the Tees enjoys, and a very boggy one – offering little encouragement to anyone who tries to follow its early track from the first swelling stream of the headwaters. It gathers strength very rapidly and in a few miles has become more river than stream and soon reaches its first bridge crossing (NY760339), and the curious might wonder why anyone would want to creat a substantial bridge in such a remote area. The answer is to be found underground in lead ore: there is a mine close by the river and the Cross Fell smelter was at work in the early nineteenth century. Now there is a definite path to walk on the hillside to the north of the river, linking a string of old mine sites and ending at the first major example of man's interference with the natural course of the river. It has been dammed to create the immense Cow Green Reservoir.

The next major change in the river comes from a natural feature, the Whin Sill. Hard, igneous rock has thrust its way through the softer sedimentary rocks, and the river has steadily eaten away and eroded the latter while making little impression on the former. The result is, indeed, very sill-like – two great, sudden drops that create the impressive falls of Cauldron Snout and High Force, made all the more impressive by their wild settings. Below Cauldron Snout, walkers can again enjoy splendid riverside walks, often in narrow rock-defined gorges or turn to tracks over the high moor.

Leaving the moorland region the river carves an ever broader valley. Settlements become more frequent; at first isolated farms, then hamlets and finally the substantial village of Middleton-in-Teesdale, a place with solid houses of local stone, which owes its existence in part to the local lead mines and partly to the situation. Here the Lune – not connected to the better known river in Lancashire – meets the Tees, so that the meeting of two valleys provides also a meeting of roads, and the first really important river bridge. Gradually the river eases its way out of the narrow confines of the hills, spreading itself and creating an ever lusher environment. Riverside walks now offer a quite different experience – woodland closes in on banks as the river reaches its first major town, Barnard Castle. The Romans came this way, pushing their road across the river at this point, and a Norman lord, Bernard de Baliol, chose the rocky promontory above the river to build his castle in the twelfth century, around which the market town grew.

Barnard Castle marks a very definite change in the character of the river. Teesdale comes to an end as the river saunters out into the industrial region based on the Durham coalfield. It makes its way south of Darlington, indulging in ever more extravagent bends and twists. Neasham (LR93, NZ3310) and Middleton St George (NZ3413) are a mere 2 miles (3 km) apart by direct line, but are separated by 9 miles (14 km) of convoluted river. We are entering a region that has its own charms, but is probably of less interest to walkers than the higher reaches – a state of affairs which is true of many rivers. But it does have some remarkable features not least its bridges. At Yarm (NZ418132) the railway line from Northallerton to Stockton approaches the river on a long viaduct of 41 brick arches that carries it above the town and then goes over the river itself on two tall arches of stone. By the time Middlesbrough is reached, the Tees has broadened to the point where shipyards once lined its banks, starting at Stockton. Bridges now needed to take account of the passage of the ships and the solution found here was the bizarre transporter bridge. Cars and passengers are carried over on a cradle suspended from a high overhead gantry. We are now very much in the industrial area of Teesside which continued all the way to the sea. This is emphatically not an area for country walks by the river, but we have stayed with the Tees simply to show the immense contrast between the high moorland where it was born and the world of refineries and factories where it ends. The Tees is by no means unique in showing this immense variety – not just in terms of scenery to be met along the way, but also in the multiple uses which man has made of its waters.

There are two very obvious examples of man's intervention: using the power of water to work machinery and using the river for transport. The water mill has been around since Roman times, and was once a vital part of community life. At first the water wheel was used almost exclusively for driving the machinery of a

On this Cornish stream the water tumbles over a weir on the left, while sluice gates to the right control the flow into an artificial channel, eventually to turn a mill wheel at Cotehele.

It is easy to think of watermills such as Sturminster Newton as being no more than picturesque additions to the scenery, but they were once vital to the local community.

grain mill. But as the centuries went by its versatility increased: there were textile mills, gunpowder mills, there were the great pounding hammers of the forges and, in a more modern context, the turbine for the generation of electrical power. We shall be looking at this aspect of river life in more detail in Chapter 8.

The rivers of Britain have been used for transport for thousands of years. The blue stones that were taken from the Preseli Mountains in Wales to build the great circle at Stonehenge were almost certainly brought to the site by being rafted up the Wiltshire Avon. There is an element of conjecture here, but archaeologists have found remains of actual boats, built as long ago as the Bronze Age, that ended their days sunk in the mud flats of the Humber. So it is not surprising to find evidence of river transport on a walk: what is sometimes surprising is to realise just how far inland boats traded until comparatively recently. The upper reaches of the Wye were once busy with boats which left the Severn at Chepstow, swept up past the romantic ruins of Tintern Abbey under Brockweir Bridge and were still reaching as high as Bigsweir Bridge (LR162, SO538051) in the early years of this century. Once they went even higher, and there are traces of a towing path where men walked, hauling the boats behind them all the way to Monmouth. There are memories of the past all along the river – old wharves can still be seen very clearly beside Brockweir Bridge, while at Tintern itself all the river uses come together. Next to the former railway bridge over the river is an old corn mill, converted to a wood-turning factory that continued in use until the 1950s and beside that is a small dock – water transport meets water power.

The Wye must always have been a horrendously difficult river to navigate, and as you walk its banks it is difficult to believe that anything bigger and less manageable than a canoe ever used its swirling waters. Other rivers were tamed to a greater or lesser extent. The earliest method was by 'flash locks', not unlike a modern weir as the water was dammed by moveable sluice gates and, when there was a good head of water, the gates were removed and boats either swept down on the flood or were slowly winched upstream. There are very few reminders of those days, but on many rivers we can still see their replacements – the pound locks. Anyone who walks along the bank of the Thames, often following the old towpath, will be familiar with the locks. They are popular places for stopping and staring as the boats – almost invariably pleasure boats these days – either drop down between the dripping walls or rise up in a flurry of foam.

It is so much a part of the river scene that we take it for granted, and think of it as a process that in its essentials has not changed for centuries. But if you stop and look you will find a far more complex pattern than is immediately obvious. Take perhaps the most famous lock on the river, Boulter's, near Maidenhead (LR175, SU9082). It has gone through a whole series of transformations. In the early eighteenth century, there was a watermill here, and the miller built a weir across the river to hold back the flow and divert the stream for his mill – which was bad news for boatmen. A flash lock was built at the new weir and down that they sped. Then in 1772 a conventional lock was built in the cutting that took water past Taplow Mill on the east bank. Half a century later, a whole new cutting made just for boats was constructed beside the west bank and a second lock installed – and that is the Boulter's Lock we see today. It follows a pattern repeated time and again up the whole river. A weir holds back the water, which can be controlled by sluices. An artificial cutting is dug with a lock in the middle, so that boats can rise and fall in a gentle, dignified manner rather than having to cope with the rapids and shallows of the natural river or the alarms and frights of the thundering waters of the flash lock.

Weirs feature throughout much of the river system of Britain, and wherever they are spotted on a walk you can be sure that something was happening at that spot at some time or other. Sometimes one finds a mill converted into a house, but still retaining traces of its old sluices, or the mill may be reduced to a pile of rubble and only the leat

Paddle gear on the old Pocklington Canal.

that once brought the water to the turning wheel remains. More rarely there may be indications that this was once part of a now forgotten navigation system. But there will be something of interest, if one knows how to look for it.

The towpath of the Rochdale Canal provides a footpath across the Pennines to the heart of Manchester. The canal is now being restored.

There was a limit to the navigational improvements that could be made to Britain's rivers and by the mid-eighteenth century that limit had been reached. The answer was to link the natural rivers by artificial canals and in a period of little more than half a century, thousands of miles of these waterways were dug, many with impressive engineering features: tall aqueducts swept high over valleys, tunnels burrowed for miles under the earth; canals rose up on high banks or sank deep down into dark cuttings. They all had one thing in common: they were built in the pre-motor age, so there had to be a towpath for the horse. In recent years, canal towpaths have been recognised as valuable long-distance routes for walks: the Grand Union Canal, for example, provides a continuous footpath from the heart of London into the middle of Birmingham. They can be wholly rural, like the delightful Brecon and Abergavenny Canal, which runs for virtually its whole length through the Brecon Beacons National Park. Or they can sneak up on the backs of towns and insinuate themselves into cities: the Leeds and Liverpool Canal provides a green route right into the very heart of Leeds. It is in the nature of canals that they keep clear of the steepest hills, or when they are faced by severe slopes either bend round their edge or take the very gentlest uphill route available by a series of locks. They are particularly good paths for those who have problems with climbs, but there can be difficulties, particularly where towpaths are badly maintained. Long tunnels represent a special problem: but even in the working days, there was generally a route over the hill, along which the horse was led while the men legged their way in the dark, pushing the boat along by walking their feet along the sides or roof of the tunnel.

As well as the waterways still in use there are hundreds of miles of canal that have been abandoned, but which still provide walks, as the former towpath has remained as a right of way. Some, such as the Somerset Coal Canal, are being cleaned up so that walkers can enjoy the remains: the bridges, the empty lock chambers and all the reminders of a working past. One particularly attractive section can be traced from Midford (LR172, ST7660) along the valley of the Cam Brook, beautiful, green and peaceful, but leading it seems to an impossible climb up the hills. Soon locks appear, but still the task seems insurmountable, then suddenly the canal goes through a hairpin bend to end up high above the valley at beautiful Combe Hay. And those who take this walk often find themselves faced with a great many questions – not all of which have an obvious answer, which will be left to those who come this way to find out for themselves. One of the appeals of walking derelict canals is that one often comes across quite puzzling structures. Staying with the West Country and moving down to the Grand

The canal age was also the age of the first cast-iron bridges. As the waterway is a standard width, standard bridges could be cast, and this elegant design can be found all along the northern Oxford Canal.

Western Canal, it is possible to follow the line westward from Nynehead along the Tone valley, meeting all kinds of curiosities, including the cast-iron trough of an old aqueduct. But the most intriguing feature is to be found in an overgrown wooded area (LR181 ST144218), a mass of masonry and brick that looks a bit like a lock but is not. This is the remains of a boat lift. There were two caissons – a bit like oversized bathtubs on rails – joined together by chains. A boat going uphill floated into the lower caisson – extra water was added to the upper caisson until it began to fall, and as it did so the linked caisson with the boat started to rise. There is a great deal to be said for a walk on a route which goes through a peaceful, rural world but carries such memories of a busy past. Disused canals are not invariably shown as such on the OS maps, so a little research is sometimes needed to locate them. It is all the more rewarding afterwards to come across incontrovertible evidence – perhaps gently rusting paddle gear in a bush or an old mile post – and know that you got it right.

Navigable canals are not the only form of artificial waterways. Drainage ditches can be works of just as great a magnitude, and some do in fact become navigable as well, even if this is generally a secondary consideration. Maps of much of East Anglia have a fascinating story to tell. The south-eastern quarter of Landranger 113 shows the flat lands to the south of the Humber – and flat is certainly the word for a map which shows not a single contour line between the edge of the Wolds and the sea. What it does show is a land covered by the straight blue line of dykes and the caterpillar-like tracks of flood banks. This is an area where land has been reclaimed since Saxon times. The main A1031 takes a course that seems inexplicably erratic, full of incomprehensible right-angled bends. In fact for much of its length it follows an Anglo-Saxon sea bank, and villages such as Marshchapel and Grainthorpe were already well established by the time the Normans came.

What does such an area offer to the walker? Is it no more than a series of footpaths running in straight lines over a flat, empty landscape? In fact, it is a good deal better than that. This is an area of eerie charms, of immense contrasts between the regular patterns of the land with its geometric lines of lanes and ditches and fields, reminiscent of a Mondrian painting, and the immense sky of changing cloud patterns. Reason tells us that the sky is the sky, neither bigger in one place than another nor more varied, but it is true that in these flat lands it seems vast and more compelling. The eye is constantly drawn upwards. It is not surprising that if one looks down it is the name of the Dutch artist Mondrian that comes to mind, but gazing upwards, conjures the no less dramatic great cloudscapes of the East Anglian painter Constable.

One area which offers a unique opportunity to compare the ancient wetland with its more modern counterpart is centred on Wicken Fen, one of the last areas of undrained fen in the region (LR154, TL5570), now in the care of the

National Trust. Here one can find the whole history of the region laid out on view. Five thousand years ago, there were forests here, but the climate grew wetter, the sea bit ever deeper into the land, rivers swelled and the forest became a swamp. The great trees died – some to re-emerge as bog-oaks that can still be seen – others to rot away to peat. It became a land of dark pools, sedge and reed, but the surviving fens had their value: reed for thatch, pools for fish and wildfowl, peat for fuel. Causeways or droves give access to the wetland, and here in the fen is a reminder of Dutch influence in the drainage process, a little wooden windmill, or smock mill, which was used to turn a simple scoop wheel for drainage. All round this evocative area is the more modern farm landscape, offering a whole range of watery themes. Ditches or lodes – at least one of which, Reach Lode, was begun by the Romans – lead down to the River Cam, with its navigation locks and busy traffic of pleasure boats. It is an area full of interest, and walking through it gives one an insight into the importance of the underlying landscape features. A walk from Wicken down to the Cam and back down one of the lodes reveals a very modest rise of land above the fens, just enough for major settlements, Reach, Burwell and the two Swaffhams to find a foothold.

Similar walks can be made in other wetland areas, such as the Somerset Levels, where again there is a pattern of ditches and banks created centuries ago, and where every rise has its settlement. Here, too, one can find the nineteenth-century equivalents of the Fenland windmills, a succession of brick buildings that once housed steam engines, one of which, Westonzoyland pumping station (LR182, ST340328), has been preserved and returned to working order. But a landscape carved by straight ditches does not always indicate a pattern of drainage: sometimes quite the contrary. The medieval change from arable to pasture created a problem of finding fodder for the growing flocks, and one answer in the river valleys was the water meadow.

At its simplest this involved damming a river or stream and allowing the water to flood out through sluices and channels over the surrounding grassland. This was done at the beginning of the year to encourage growth, and later the process was reversed and the water channelled away again. The system is no longer used, but the remains of it can be seen in many areas such as the valley of the Avon below Salisbury. Here one can experience all the rich contrasts that make river valleys so exciting. In the area around Breamore, for example, (LR184, SU1617) one can walk over wooded hills passing through clumps of mature oak and sweet chestnut and then reach an area which looks as if it has been dropped in from the fens. This is an area of natural beauty, but also an environment which owes much to man's intervention. This has its own fascination, but walkers who want something altogether wilder will probably want to turn away from the valleys and set off for the hills.

Two lodes meet at a simple footbridge at the edge of Wicken Fen.

The Cuillins at Sligachan, Skye.

Chapter 8

THE UPLANDS

For many of us, the hills and mountains represent the ultimate escape, the sloughing off of the cares of the working world, the removal from the trappings of a mechanised, mechanical civilisation. Those who have once felt the pull of the hills can imagine little better than the sense of freedom of reaching a lonely summit, where, even if the works of man are in sight, they are so reduced in scale that it seems that all one has to do is reach out a hand, pluck a house from the distant landscape and pop it away in a pocket. Looking back over the years of walking, time and again it is the high-level walks that rush back with their memories: standing on the long ridge of the Cuillin Hills of Skye, clambering up to the winter summit of Snowdon, when ice and snow had stopped the trains and kept the tourists at bay or, more modestly, reaching the third of the Pennine three peaks at the end of a long day's walk. The British hills and mountains may seem puny when set against the immensity of the Himalayas, but they have their own majesty and I, for one, would not trade the hills of Lakeland for the world's greatest peaks.

There is, however, no denying that Britain does not have high mountains when measured on a European, let alone a world, scale. Ben Nevis reaches scarcely more than a quarter of the altitude of the summit of Mont Blanc. But the relatively small scale of our landscape can lead walkers to underestimate the problems of walking the British uplands, and each year the accident statistics show that too many do just that. Often, accidents happen – in fact, almost invariably accidents happen – as the result of ignorance. No one wants to suggest that walking in the British hills is like setting off on a suicide mission, but there are very real dangers. The good news is that they can be avoided.

Paradoxically, the greatest danger lies not in the hills themselves, but in the weather. The generally accepted rule is that Britain's hills qualify as mountains when they top the 3000-foot (1000-metre) mark, and that sets their summits at an altitude well above the lowest possible cloud base. Clouds present a double hazard to the walker. The most obvious one is that you can no longer see where you are going. From what has already been said it should be clear that the truest friends in these circumstances are maps and compass. But whereas taking the wrong route in the valleys can be an inconvenience, it can be a disaster in the mountains. It is absolutely essential to be aware of the presence of cliffs and crags. Tens of thousands of walkers make their way up Snowdon each year, many of them taking the easiest route, the Llanberis Path, that roughly follows the line of the mountain railway. Yet stray a short way from this route and you are on the Snowdon Ranger Path, which passes directly above the awesome rock faces of Clogwyn D'ur Arddu, which present some of the greatest challenges to rock climbers that Britain has to offer. On a fine, bright day there is no problem, but when cloud sits on the summit and everything is lost from view in a cold, dank impenetrable mist it is all too easy to make a mistake, and such weather can arrive very suddenly, even in the middle of summer. Winter presents a quite different set of problems. Whatever the weather may be at the foot of the mountain, it is virtually certain that there will be snow on the summit and that the rocks will be encased in black ice. This means that even the easiest route to the summit must be treated with caution, while those routes which are quite challenging in summer – such as the path up the dramatic, spiny Crib Goch ridge – will demand the skills and equipment of the mountaineer rather than the casual rambler. This may seem very obvious, but it is truly astonishing how many people are unaware of such fundamentals. On my own last winter visit to Snowdon, I met a couple coming up from Llanberis, dressed in shorts and plastic sandals, who took a good deal of convincing that the temperature at the top was below zero.

At least, the routes up and down Snowdon are so well used that they are clearly defined, which is not necessarily true of other hills and mountains. It is generally true that more accidents happen during descents than during climbs. If bad weather clamps down on the way up, it is generally an easy matter to turn and retrace one's steps to safety. It is when mist and cloud settle on the summit that is easy to become disorientated and miss the secure route down. One of the commonest mistakes made by the inexperienced is to argue that as water runs down hill, all one has to do is locate a stream and follow it to the valley. But although hill streams invariably end up at the lower level, they certainly do not always take the most comfortable route down. A stream may burble along reassuringly for a while and then plunge suddenly over a rock face in a high cascade. There really is only one safe answer: know where the path is and be very sure you know how to find it.

Bad weather in the hills makes route-finding difficult, but it brings other problems as well. In winter temperatures can drop alarmingly, and even in summer a sudden cooling can have severe effects on those who set out expecting no more than a stroll in the sun. Clouds do not just reduce visibility drastically, they are also unpleasantly cold and wet when experienced from the inside, sapping energy at an often alarming rate. Being caught in cloud on even a mode hill can be a frightening experience, but it need not be. There are simple rules to follow. The first is to get a local weather forecast, and plan your walk accordingly. The second is to assume that the weather forecast, however good, might just possibly be wrong. No one ever suffered harm from having too much wet weather gear in the rucksack. Next, plan your route thoroughly. Start by studying the map and make very sure that you understand it.

A popular circular walk begins at the Old Dungeon Ghyll Hotel at the end of the road up the Langdale Valley (LR90, NY286061) and follows a track known as The Band which climbs the hills to the south, up Bow Fell which commands immense views of the surrounding mountains, then passes round lonely Angle Tarn for a return on the opposite, northern side of the valley. This is a seemingly comfortable 6-mile (10-km) walk but involves climbing from the valley floor at an elevation of about 250 feet (80 metres) to a summit of over 2700 feet (900 metres). Applying Naismith's rule that should make 2½ hours for covering the distance, plus another hour and a half for the height climbed – making 4 hours in all. A short stroll has already become quite a serious walk. But that is only a part of the story. The climb is not just a considerable climb, but a very steep one as well, while the crinkly black lines indicate a profusion of crags, which in turn suggest the probability – if not the certainty – of there being a good deal of loose stone or scree on the slopes. So now we have added rough terrain to the equation. Above The Band, the path follows an undulating ridge, with cliffs to either side, before the last climb to the summit. Then comes an equally steep descent, which is over similarly rough ground and demands care. By now, it should be obvious that this is really quite a demanding excursion, even in fine weather. In bad weather the path will certainly be shrouded in cloud – and in winter the route can only be undertaken by those who are really experienced in winter hill walking and fully equipped for the job. It is not to be undertaken lightly, and there is one further point to bear in mind. This is a walk in entirely open country – no shelter, no trees, no stopping places for a pint or a cup of tea – and it is lonely country. If something should go wrong, there will be no passers-by to help. Always make certain that someone knows where you are going and when you expect to return.

No one wants to sound like nanny, wagging an admonitory finger and telling the children to be careful and not do anything silly. The whole point of going into the high hills is to enjoy the freedom and to take entire responsibility for one's own actions – and that means having the right to take risks. There is nothing wrong with this – but it is imperative to know just what the risks are and so be able to assess them. I have, in the past, been one of a rescue party who had the miserable task of carrying back the horribly broken body of a walker who had plunged over cliffs at a summit ridge – not so very different from the ridge at Bow Fell. No one would wish to have, let alone repeat, such an experience. The mountains are full of deceptions: a gully which might seem a useful short cut to a summit can close in and be blocked off, so that suddenly a walk becomes a scramble and then imperceptibly a real climb. Slopes can steepen and a short cut descent can be all too short. There is nothing more exhilarating than a first-rate walk in the mountains, and no walk with more potential dangers: and the two are inseparable. Overcoming dangers and difficulties adds immensely to the pleasure of the occasion, and gives a sense of real achievement. No one who loves the mountains wants to see rules and regulations, danger signs and warning plaques, or even, worst of all, safety fences above crags and gulleys. There will always be accidents, but individual walkers can do a great deal to make sure that they themselves are not in the statistics.

The mountainous regions of Great Britain may be modest when graded simply in terms of altitude but they do offer a real sense of wilderness. Snowdonia the Lakes and the Highlands and islands of Scotland are deservedly popular, and there are regions which can seem wholly remote and untouched. Few places are wilder than the north-west of Scotland, where mountains rise out of a primitive landscape, a place of desolate beauty, of rock-scarred moor, speckled with pools of peaty water like basins of chocolate sauce. Here is a truly ancient land. The silvery-grey rocks that add sparkle to the great expanse of peat were laid down as part of a great plain that covered the area some 600 million years ago. This in turn was covered over by sandstone, thousands of feet thick. Gradually the softer upper layers eroded, leaving the mountains that rise so dramatically, and none more so than the double peaks of Suilven (LR15, NC1517) which when seen from the west rises sheer as a vast, shapely cone. This is an astonishing landscape for walkers, but not comfortable and never easy.

Such wholly remote regions have a unique appeal, and though there are not many of them and they occupy a comparatively small area of the country as a whole, they are well worth searching out. Even in such popular places as Skye – made even more accessible to tourists with the building of a bridge to the mainland – it is possible to find magnificent mountain scenery and airy solitudes. Here is the greatest hill walk in Britain, the immense ridge of the Cuillin hills, a walk that climbs up from sea level and then rarely drops below a height of 2700 feet (900 metres) – except that it is not really a walk at all. The ridge is bare rock, and includes sections which require genuine rock-climbing skills – including the famous Inaccessible Pinnacle, easy enough, in fact, to a climber, but definitely not for the inexperienced. The ridge remains, sadly, out of bounds to the ordinary walker, so it might perhaps seem a little unfair to dwell on its glories.

But you do not have to rope up and ascend something as ominous sounding as the Crack of Doom, one of the great scenic climbs of the region, to enjoy

Clouds sweep over the Cuillin ridge, with its jagged outlines of summits and pinnacles. The ridge walk is arguably the finest high-level route in Britain – but not one for the inexperienced.

The Cuillins. A walk from Glen Brittle (LR32, NG4121) across the moor can take you to the heart of the mountains, to Coire Làgan, where the little loch its ringed by high cliffs, and a great tongue of scree shoots down from the ramparts of Sgurr Alasdair. It is as well to remember that not every walk in the hills has to reach a summit to be immensely enjoyable. But then, neither is it necessary to choose the region's highest mountains to find truly dramatic scenery. A rocky ridge, with west facing cliffs, runs right up the northern end of Skye, from just north of Portree almost as far as the northern tip. There are spectacular sites along the way, including the isolated pinnacle, the Old Man of Storr (LR23, NG500540), but it reaches its true climax at the Quiraing (NG4569). Here a path leads up to a fantastical landscape of rock pinnacles and shattered crags, at the heart of which lies a great grassy amphitheatre.

The mountains of the Lake District and the Scottish Highlands owe much of their appeal to being thought of as 'natural' landscapes. The stone walls creep up the sides of a Lakeland valley, but above them the crags and hillsides seem wholly untouched by man. This is true only of the highest peaks; elsewhere the landscape bears the marks of human history. In the distant past, the Lakeland hills were heavily wooded and much of the Highlands was blanketed in forests of birch and pine. Man changed that, first by clearing the trees, then by allowing his flocks to roam free over the hills, demolishing young saplings before they had a chance to develop. Landranger 51, Loch Tay, looks as if it covers an area

The path runs below rocky slopes to reach the extraordinary array of towers and buttresses, like a giant's fortress, of the Quiraing, Skye.

absolutely made for 'get-away-from-it-all' walking in the hills. There are hardl any roads, very few settlements – just mile after mile of hill and loch. The hig point of the whole region is Ben Lawers (LR51, NN6341) with a summit over 2500 feet (720 metres) that towers above Loch Tay. It is easily accessibl from a visitor centre by tracks that lead up over Beinn Ghlas and then follow ridge to the summit – a popular and very rewarding walk. Yet there is ample ev dence of how this landscape was transformed by the hungry flocks. Out on th mountain's flanks are the remains of shielings, temporary summer homes for th herdsmen who tended the animals, cattle mainly, until well into the nineteent century. Today the sheep roam all over the mountain, munching away quite con tentedly, and wholly unaware of their part in creating a much loved landscape One of the truly great wilderness areas can be found in the far north-west c Scotland, a vast empty landscape of hillocks and lochans flanked by spectacula peaks, known as Reay Forest. Once this was the home of the Clan MacKay, bu in 1828 it was bought up by George Levenson-Gower and thousands of familie were evicted, their crofts abandoned and the area devoted to sheep. It was ju one episode in the infamous story of the Highland Clearances which saw who communities betrayed for the profit of the absentee landlord or the pleasure c the sportsman. Those who walk this lovely, desolate land will see little more tha piles of stones to mark what were once traditional communities.

It is of interest to see how much of the land has been shaped by man, but most walkers who go to the mountains are more likely to be impressed by the immensity of natural forces that shaped the scenery long before man appeared. The coarse gabbro of the Cuillins, wonderfully rough and adhesive for climbing, was formed deep in the earth's crust to emerge and solidify aeons ago. It is totally different in texture from, say, the limestone of the Pennine hills, with its obvious laminations, caused not by the bubbling up of minerals in an ancient volcano, but the laying down of sediments in a long-vanished sea. So the rocks of the Cuillins stand proud along their high ridge, while the limestone wears away and weathers to form the typical 'stepped' slopes and escarpment edges which give hills such as Ingleborough their distinctive profiles. The vast scooped out valleys which typify the Lake District and Snowdonia were formed by the movement of glaciers. Geology books give all this information in detail, but it is by going to these areas that one actually understands what it all means. You can feel the bright, hard, crystalline surface of the gabbro and catch an almost metallic gleam in the sun: look down from Snowdon along the Llanberis Pass and it requires very little imagination to visualise the relentless movement of a glacier, smoothing away the valley sides as it dug down deep between the mountains.

The approach to Ben Lawers. In the foreground are the ruins of a shieling, where herdsmen would spend the summer tending the grazing cattle.

The view down the Llanberis Pass from Snowdon.

The name 'upland' is not synonymous with 'mountain'. Glencoe is undeniably an area of true mountains, but the adjoining vast waste expanse of Rannoch Moor is an upland area as well – and every bit as wild. It looks, and is, inhospitable: an area of pools and lochs, wandering streams and peaty bogs, of rough tussocky grass that makes walking difficult. It has its own appeal. It is an area which few choose to explore, but those who do find an immensity of sky that one only expects to find in a region such as East Anglia: a panorama of mountains to add excitement to the view and a demanding terrain that puts the walker to the test.

The peaty wilderness of Rannoch Moor.

An upland area every bit as popular as the mountains is moorland, a term defined by the dictionary as 'unenclosed waste land', a definition which is appropriately vague, for the upland moors often have little in common apart from the name. There is a great contrast between, say, Dartmoor, with its prominent tors and the heather moors of North Yorkshire, and the differences extend beyond the scenery. They show up very clearly on the larger scale maps, such as the Outdoor Leisure maps, which are available for both areas. Spread out the Dartmoor map (OL28) and look at the side showing the northern end of the moor and what is immediately obvious is an area round the edges which contains quite sizeable settlements and a network of fields, some of which poke tentatively over the margin of the moor and creep up the slopes, while most of the western half of the map shows just one vast open space, with smaller patches of open moor also dominating to the east. The map symbols on these areas show rough grass, bracken and marsh, dotted with rocks and more substantial tors. A few rough tracks penetrate into the heart of this wilderness, but it seems a very empty land. It is however, an area where short walks present few problems. It is easy to start in the fringe and walk out into the moor, perhaps leaving South Zeal (OL28, SX6593) to reach one of the high points, Cosdon Hill, or perhaps going on to Little Hound Tor and returning via Belstone. Or one could base a walk on some of the more spectacular rock formations, perhaps linking Hound Tor (7479) to Haytor (7577) These walks guarantee open countryside, splendid views and dramatic features

They also offer, as a closer look reveals, a rich pattern of historic and prehistoric sites, from the stone rows on the flank of Cosdon Hill to the remains of a medieval village at Hound Tor.

Many walkers rise to the greater challenge of long walks over the moor, and these can be as demanding as any walks in the higher mountains. The centre of Dartmoor is open to the elements with nothing in the way of cover, and, although it may not be obvious, stands at a considerable height above sea level – seldom falling below the 1500-foot (500-metre) level. The walker is therefore as likely to be engulfed by bad weather here as in the higher mountains. When a grey, uniform stratus cloud settles low it not only produces rain, but also a very marked chilling effect, which can cause problems even in summer. Winter snows can produce very severe conditions indeed. Dartmoor also presents its own difficulties in that landmarks are very few and far between, so that route finding, even on good days, poses a challenge. There may be no great Grimpen Mire ready to swallow up horse or man, as in the famous Sherlock Holmes story, but there are some very unpleasant bogs none the less. Dartmoor remains one of the great walking areas, full of interest, but one that demands a sensible approach.

The North York Moors present a very different picture from that found on Dartmoor. The total area of the national park is huge, over 500 square miles, but it does not have the same areas of regular open upland. Instead it is eaten away and fissured by little valleys and winding dales. This provides an opportunity to create many varied walks, full of contrasts. One might start, for example, at the car park beside the upper reaches of the River Rye (OL26 SE530928). Here one finds streams running down little rocky valleys, covered in oak and birch woodland, with all around the edges small fields surrounding isolated farms. Even the field names tell of the pattern of use – the name 'Intake' crops up regularly on the fringe of the moor, denoting an area where sheep can be gathered in. Beyond them are the scattered sheepfolds. Once out on the heather moorland, however, a different use soon appears. All over the moor are rows of small circular enclosures made of dry stone walls, generally topped with moss and heather. These are the grouse butts where the shooters wait each autumn for the birds to be beaten out of the heather towards the waiting guns. The fundamental pleasure of walking these moors is not so very different from those of walking over Dartmoor, even though the terrain is so very different. There is the same sense of space and solitude, the appeals which draw so many to the hills from the Quantocks to the Highlands. But if one is looking for 'unspoiled' country, then that is harder to find. The North York map is as liberally spattered with 'working (dis)' as it is with grouse butts: Dartmoor has intriguing labels, such as 'tinner's hut' equally widely spread. Industry in one form or another seems to have invaded even the wildest places.

Disused mills line the Rochdale Canal at Hebden Bridge.

Chapter 9

THE WORKING PAST

There are some who are fascinated by the remains of the industrial past, but even those who declare themselves totally uninterested can hardly escape them. In the last chapter, we looked briefly at the wide expanses of Dartmoor. On nearby Exmoor, if anywhere, one might think oneself entirely removed from the industrial world. Yet, spread throughout the area are the remains of lead mines and copper mines, not to mention the more exotic silver and gold mines. The hills were quarried for slate and building stone and there was a wide range of rural industries, from manufacturers of agricultural machinery to woollen mills. Traces of all or any of these are likely to be encountered on a moorland walk. And this is only a part of the story, for the production centres were linked to each other and to the ports and markets by a complex transport system. The remains are there, but not always easily recognised, simply because few of the sites have been worked for a century or more.

Among the few substantial remains is the engine house of the old iron ore mine near Burrow Farm in the Brendon Hills at the edge of Exmoor, which closed down in 1883. In its day, the mine was kept open by the mighty steam engine that pumped up water from deep underground, and now only the shell of the building that housed it remains (LR181, ST008345). Nevertheless, it remains one of the most striking landscape features of the whole area. Such sites crop up time and again in areas that seem to be just the sort of wild regions most likely to appeal to walkers. So, even those who do not set out deliberately to hunt down the reminders of an industrial past are likely to come across them, whether they wish to or not.

The hunt for mineral wealth beneath the ground is one of man's oldest industrial activities. We have already seen how Neolithic man followed the richest veins of flint beneath the surface and how the Romans utilised sophisticated techniques to uncover gold ore. For walkers, however, most of the visible physical remains of mining that are encountered are unlikely to date back beyond the eighteenth century. The Industrial Revolution created a vast demand for raw materials: mineral ores, coal, building stone and slate. The extraction of minerals has a long history, and sites often have layer upon layer of history, like industrial palimpsests.

The Mendips offer a rich variety of landscapes for the walker. There are famous natural features, such as the limestone gorges, of which Cheddar is the most famous and certainly the most popular with tourists. Ebbor Gorge (LR182, ST5248) is altogether wilder and inaccessible to any but walkers, which makes it an attractive feature to include in any circuit. Looking over the 1:25 000 Explorer Map 4, all kinds of names meet the eye. Nine Barrows Lane, which does indeed almost lead up to nine round barrows. The little village of Priddy sits at a cross roads, one of which is called Petting Drove, which suggests a collecting point, and sure enough those who visit Priddy find a village of considerable charm, with a large green, which still has a shelter containing a stack of hurdles that can be erected almost in an instant to create a temporary enclosure. The contours show an undulating, hilly landscape, with no shortage of paths, so this is a good place to walk.

Perhaps one other feature might excite the curiosity. How about the spot with the extraordinary name – St Cuthbert's Swallet (ST5450)? Here one finds the remains of the very last lead smelting works in the area – which closed in 1908; but it was not usually freshly mined ore that was treated here, but slag left behind by older, less technologically developed miners. It was heated and the fumes passed through long lines of flues, where the lead condensed out. The flues can still be seen, impressive even in ruins, as a long line of tunnels. If this excites the interest, then there is not far to go to another smelt works, near Charterhouse on Mendip. The Romans came here to mine for lead, and there is still the outline of their old fort and a nearby settlement, all neatly squared off (ST5055 and 5050). The earliest miners followed the vein of ore down from the surface, carving out 'rakes', sort of man-made Cheddar gorges. All down the valley are the remains of mines, including great circular indentations, where the ore was worked, known as 'buddles', and an even more spectacular set of flues (507560) – which are a popular sunbathing spot for adders. It says a great deal about an area that has been an important industrial site that much of it is now a nature reserve. If the Mendip mining sites do nothing else, they demolish any notion that 'industrial' necessarily means ugly. Indeed, lead mines are found in some of the most attractive upland regions. In the Derbyshire Peak District the immense rakes, such as Dortlow Rake near Castleton (LR110, SK1481), are impressive landscape features. As well as the rakes, shafts were sunk to the deep ore and above them stand the crumbling remains of old engine houses, notably at Magpie Mine (LR119, SK173682).

Magpie Mine, Sheldon. Many of the surface buildings of this old lead mine survive, including the remains of two engine houses, the manager's house and a small smithy.

Mining remains are always apt to crop up on even the wildest and most picturesque walks. Long walks do not come much lonelier than the Southern Upland Way. About halfway along the route, walkers from the west coast climb up over the hills beyond Sanquhar, and there, opened out before them, is a landscape of melancholy desolation; spoil scars the hillside, man-made adits dive into the hills, and ruined buildings line the route to the old mining village of Wanlockhead. It can be a forbidding place, but it is also one of great fascination: those who break their journey here to explore for a few hours rarely regret the decision.

The Dales Way passes close by the mining area based on Grassington, and other minerals are found in equally beautiful locations. No one can walk the coastal paths of the South West and be unaware of the engine houses that mark the old tin and copper mines. Of all the mine sites that might earn the epitaph romantic, none are more so than those around Land's End, and the finest of them all must be the old Botallack Mine (LR203, SW362333), where the lower of the two engine houses clings to a seemingly impossible position on a tiny ledge halfway down the cliff face – while the mine itself once ran well out under the seabed. Cornish engine houses are as likely to appear on high moorland as they are on a cliff's edge, and are much admired – now that the smoke, the fumes, and the rumbles of underground explosions have died away. Sometimes one has to remind oneself that the search for mineral wealth could devastate a whole region.

Engine houses are an inescapable feature of the Cornish coastal path. This was the engineer's view out over the cliffs of Rinsey Head, when he could take time off from tending his vast steam engine.

We know minerals were being won and worked on Anglesey in Roman times, but it was only in the eighteenth century that the discovery was made that Parys Mountain (LR114, SH4490) was one great mass of copper ore, the mountain was subsequently attacked with immense ferocity. The heart of it was quarried out; shafts were sunk and water kept away by pump, powered first by wind then by steam. The ore was taken, smashed and separated in great settling tanks at the foot of the hill – and when there was no more ore it was simply abandoned. Today it is an extraordinary landscape, with its old tanks full of water still stained by the metals, while the once green hill is as sterile as the moon. Nothing grows in this jumble of rocks and immense caverns resembling volcano craters. A walk to Parys Mountain offers a landscape unlike anything else in Britain.

Perhaps the most widespread of all extractive activities is coal mining. Coal measures appear all over the British Isles from the lowlands of Scotland to the unlikely surroundings of the fields and orchards of Kent, from North East England to South Wales. In recent years there has been a drastic decline in coal mining, which has virtually disappeared from regions of Britain where once it was the dominant industry. As the more remote pits closed, so the communities that once depended on them dwindled and died. In the valleys of South Wales one can find, still, odd remains of pit-head gear like giant sculptures in the

The ravaged landscape of Parys Mountain, Anglesey. In the distance are the stump of an old wind-powered pump and the engine house that replaced it. The settling beds stained with ore fill the foreground.

The summit of Parys Mountain has been quarried and mined, eaten away until all that is left of a hill that was once as green as its surroundings is a sterile jumble of rocks.

landscape and rows of simple cottages, gradually decaying as once loved and tended gardens run riot. When the pits were busy, this was not everyone's favourite walking area: now they are closed, the natural beauties of the region are reappearing. For years, the River Usk seemed to divide two worlds. To the north, the shapely Sugar Loaf Mountain rose up above Abergavenny to stand sentinel over the beauties of the Black Mountains. To the south were the valleys, narrowly separated by high ridges, but each, like its neighbour, associated with dirt, smoke and work. It never was that simple a divide: there always was beauty in the valleys as well, but it is even less true now that the fires of the furnaces have died. What is left is a region that is very well worth exploring.

Walk out of Abersychan, for example, up the valley of Cwm Sychan (LR171 SO2404) and you come to all that remains of a mining hamlet and its pit, substantial remains – spoil heaps, chimney, head gear. Then one can turn to walk north to an area of splendid high moorland, up over Coity Mountain to drop down into Blaenafon, a town built on coal and iron. So important were the iron works that citizens were even buried under cast-iron gravestones.

The mine is a museum, but the grandest survivor is the old iron works where a range of blast furnaces, like bastions of a medieval fortress, line the hills (LR161 SO2409). From here the walk can go on, taking up a theme and a site mentioned earlier (p. 56), for Blaenafon had its tramway line across the Blorenge to the Brecon and Abergavenny Canal. Those who take to the valleys will find, perhaps to their surprise, that the scenery can be every bit as fine as in the more widely recognised areas of beauty, and the presence of an industrial past can actually enhance the interest and the pleasure of the walk.

The 18th-century iron works at Blaenafon. The blast furnaces are mightily impressive, as is this water balance tower, a lift used to move trucks and material between the top and foot of the furnaces.

Staying with the theme of mines and quarries, but moving on to another product as closely associated with North Wales as coal is with South Wales, we arrive at slate. Walk in Snowdonia and you cannot miss the evidence of what was once a vastly important industry. One of the most startling sights during the walk up Snowdon itself is the view across to the hillside above Llyn Peris where you can see how a whole mountainside has been eaten away to create terraces linked by inclines. It is scarcely possible to walk any of the hills in the area without coming across similar scenes, if not always quite so dramatic. Perhaps the most exciting remains are of long-abandoned mines in remote areas. In the hills to the north of Porthmadog, on the slopes of Moel Hebog (LR115, SH5745) are the old Gorseddau quarries. Further down the hill, water from the Afon Henwy was brought by aquaduct to work the machinery of the Cwmystradllyn slate mill. It rises like a majestic Gothic church, above a mountain of shattered slate. It can seem sometimes as if half the mountains of North Wales have been mined and quarried to produce enough slate for every rooftop in Britain.

This is not meant to be a complete list of such activities. One of the appeals of these remains is the variety. You can walk to the south west from Beddgelert to reach Cwmystradllyn – walk east and you reach the no less interesting remains of the Sygun copper mine. It is very rare to reach such sites and not find something of interest – old machinery left behind to rust, surface buildings, shafts and adits. They are as poignant in their way as the humps and hollows of a deserted village set among green fields.

Mining and quarrying are fundamental activities, essential for industrial progress, but walking among their remains will suggest connections with other technologies. There is the most obvious one: the material so laboriously gained is used for something, as at Blaenafon where the iron works are set on the coalfield which provided fuel for the furnaces. And that, too, suggests an important point: in many processes fuel is the most significant factor. Because smelting used many tons of coal for each ton of ore, it always made sense to take the ore to the coalfield. So you rarely find smelters in Cornwall, which has the ore but no coal – the copper smelters are over the water in South Wales along with the tinplate works. It also explains why Cornwall had such a crucial role to play in the development of steam power. The steam engine was absolutely essential in draining deep mines, and in an area without its own fuel supplies, every gain in efficiency was doubly valuable. When you change an element in the industrial equation, you produce far reaching changes in communities and ultimately in the landscape. When coke replaced charcoal in the blast furnaces of foundries, the age-old industry based on charcoal from local woods began to decline. Hence we have the abandoned hammer pond in the Weald of Kent and crumbling furnace remains still to be found in the wooded hills above the Wye valley between Monmouth and Chepstow. Similar changes in technology brought major shifts in emphasis in that other widespread activity: the making of textiles.

The spinning of raw material into yarn and the weaving of cloth go back into prehistory. By medieval times, there was a well established pattern where women spun the yarn – hence the name 'spinster' – while the work of weaving on the loom largely went to the men. This is a very crude description of a complex process, but it gives the broad picture. Virtually the only part of the process that was in any sense industrialised was fulling, in which the cloth was washed clear of grease and pounded by hammers to felt it, creating a closer weave. The fulling mill was once as common as the grain mill – and one mill could house the big water-powered hammers at one stage of its life, and these could at some stage be replaced by the more familiar grindstones at another time. Anyone coming across an old watermill on a walk has no means of knowing what its function might have been at any particular time in the past. But that does not mean that all traces of this early period of textile making have vanished. The women workers could spin almost anywhere – the spinning wheel is easily moved. They could spin in the house or sit outside on a good day, so there are no physical traces of their efforts. Weaving was different. The makers of broad cloth worked at a wide loom which required a great deal of space, and the

Weavers' cottages rise up behind the Methodist graveyard at Heptonstall. The coming of steam took work from the village down to the mills beside the new Rochdale Canal at Hebden Bridge (see *page 128*).

intricate work also needed to be well lit. The result was the development of a type of house designed round the requirements of the loom. They are still to be found in many parts of Britain, some instantly recognisable, others needing an expert eye to detect them. The most obvious feature is the large window or windows. In

As water power gave way to steam power, so many of the old textile mills that straddled the hill streams were abandoned. This former fulling mill is at Cheesden Lumb near Rochdale.

Scotland, where there is a tradition of building single storey cottages, the only give-away tends to be a window at one end of the house that is twice the size of the rest. In two other areas where woollen cloth weaving was concentrated, the West of England and the northern counties of Yorkshire and Lancashire, the weaver's cottage is widespread and easily distinguishable. In general the looms were on the upper floor, illuminated by a long row of small-paned windows.

It is perhaps only of minor interest to many to be able to spot a weaver's cottage, but it does help to make sense of the landscape. The Colne Valley Circular Walk stays, as one would expect, very much to the high moorland that rises to either side of the valley itself that runs down from the Pennine ridge towards Huddersfield. But up here one finds weavers' cottages in great profusion, some still lived in, others left to fall into ruin. What is very clear is that this was work which was once spread throughout a whole region, and that, in turn, helps to explain the multiplicity of old packhorse routes and ways. Then came technological change, and in its wake a whole new pattern of development. It began not with wool, but with cotton, when the first stages of preparation were taken out of the home, away from the cottage, and passed on to the new machines of the mill. Instead of the housewife working a treadle with her foot to turn a spindle, the water wheel was used to turn hundreds of spindles to do the same job. So, the textile industry moved down from the hillside cottages to the swift streams of the valleys.

The water wheel has a unique characteristic: it takes its power from the fall of a stream, but can pass that power on, with scarcely diminished force, to another mill further down the valley. Even when the process is improved by damming the stream to create a mill pond, from which the water can be released in a regulated flow, it is still possible for one quite modest stream to serve a whole string of mills. In former times, when the word 'mill' was most likely to be synonymous with 'grain mill', there was no need for such a profusion of mills: but in the world of textiles things were very different. Streams were pressed into service to supply the power for mills which followed each other down the valleys with the regularity of a staircase. Look at a map of the Pennines at the Lancashire-Yorkshire border and the hints are there. The Cheesden Brook runs down Deeply Vale (LR109, SD8214) and the stream is shown as bulging out in a series of lakes and ponds. It does not look like a natural phenomenon and nor is it. What you are seeing on the map is a set of mill ponds, and a walk down this lonely moorland valley is a fascinating glimpse into the importance of water power two centuries ago. The most impressive survivor is the old Cheesden Lumb Mill, built in 1786 as a fulling mill, the only survivor with substantial remains of over a dozen mills threading the length of the stream. Once again, one can walk this remote valley and scarcely be aware of its history – yet knowing that history adds immensely to the pleasures of the walk.

If one had to choose just one walk to demonstrate the gradual movement from home-based cottage industry through an industry based on the power of the water wheel and on to the greatest change of all, the introduction of the power of the steam engine, one could do no better then turn to the Calder valley. Perched on a hill, high above the valley at the edge of a wide expanse of moorland is the village of Heptonstall (LR103, SO9828). The valley clusters its buildings together in a tight knot, but everywhere there is evidence of old prosperity. Here are weavers' cottages galore, a sixteenth-century cloth hall where the local weavers could sell their ware, and that great mark of local dignity, a grammar school founded in the seventeenth century. This is a village to explore, a place to linger – and a place that speaks of wealth won by everyday activities, for the local people were able to raise the funds in the eighteenth century to build a quite splendid Methodist church, the oldest church of that denomination still in use. From here the paths spread out over the moor to Burnley and down a cobbled way to the valley and the route to Halifax.

Cottages such as these can be found throughout the southern Pennines. They are distinguished by the long rows of 'weavers' windows' on the upper floor which lit the work of the loom.

But take the splendid open walk over the hill and drop down to the valley of Hebden Water, and the next stage of local history is revealed. Here the new spinning mills of the eighteenth century were located. One of these, Gibson Mill (SD972298), survives with its vast mill pond, a solid edifice of enduring stone. Others have succumbed – now only identifiable by the flat platforms of their foundations and the remnants of weirs and sluices. Just as the cottage industry declined when faced with the commercial superiority of the water-powered mills, so the latter succumbed in their turn to the power of steam. Released from the need for fast flowing water, the steam mill builders moved into a new, more desirable location, where the turnpike road and the Rochdale Canal offered cheap, efficient transport. A new centre grew up at Hebden Bridge, where mills jostled in the valley floor, and the houses were pushed up to precarious perches on the steep hillside. It is a story that was repeated time and again, and it is one that can be traced through many a walk that combines the delights of high moorland with those of the river valley. Such a walk shows how a whole pattern of development changed, so that one old industrial centre is scarcely recognisable as such, and seems the very model of an unspoiled rural village, while another, which grew up at its expense, still seems an almost aggressively industrial focal point.

This chapter is not meant to be a potted history of industrial development. Instead it has two principal aims. The first is to show that there are very few areas of this country untouched by the industrial world. Indeed, we do not think of some of the sites as industrial developments at all; although, to take another example, the distilleries with their distinctive pagoda-roofed maltings that pop up at regular intervals along the beautiful valley of the Spey are as much a part of the industrial world as any forge or cotton mill. The second, and in a sense more pressing, objective, is to demonstrate that this is not a world to be shunned by the walker. If there is one area where I would take the enthusiastic walker to show that an industrial world can be as attractive as the wildest moorland, it would be to the region of the West of England, once famous for its woollen mills. Many have gone, but a good few, in an extraordinary variety of styles, still survive. The old mill at Malmesbury by the Avon has the elegance of a Georgian country house; Egypt Mill at Nailsworth has the rough charm of a Cotswold cottage; Ebley Mill is built like a French chateau; while St Mary's Mill could almost be mistaken for one of the grander stately homes. And most of these can be found within walking distance of the lovely Cotswold Way.

Avon Mill, Malmesbury was built to spin woollen yarn in 1790 and has the simple, easy grace of its age. The sluices controlled the water flow for the mill.

The magnificent church at Chipping Campden.

Chapter 10

SETTLEMENTS

t is possible – but not easy – to walk all day in Britain without encountering a hamlet or village. For many walkers, the village makes an obvious stopping place for rest and refreshment, whether for a welcome lunch break or somewhere to relax at the end of a long, hard day. But it is easy to think of the village as little more than an interruption to the walk, or perhaps to note that it is 'picturesque' and leave it at that. In fact, however, a village has much in common with the surrounding landscape: it will generally carry the physical traces of an often long history.

The obvious starting point is the church, if only because its tower or spire is likely to be the first landmark we see from a distance: the defining feature. The church is also likely to be the oldest building in the region, though it is very unlikely to have survived the centuries without substantial alterations – the Victorians, in particular, were much given to 'restoring' churches out of all recognition. Even so, it is rare to find a church that does not have something to say about the village or even the area as a whole. Many of them carry the message of former glories. This is particularly true of the so called 'wool churches' of areas such as East Anglia and the Cotswolds. Here one finds quite modest towns and villages blessed with extraordinarily sumptious churches reflecting a wealth that reached a peak in the late Middle Ages. Others, in different regions, might simply reflect the patronage of some local grandee. There are, at a rough estimate, some 18,000 parish churches in England alone, so it is not surprising to find an immense diversity, which ensures that they will always be of interest.

Some view churches purely in terms of their architectural style: admiring the rugged simplicity of Saxon work, the massive solidity of the Normans as compared to the airy lightness and elaborate detail of the Perpendicular or the comparative austerity of the classical. Others delight in churches for the surprises they can bring, the way in which what would seem initially to be yet another simple church can turn out on closer acquaintance to be something quite extraordinary. One walk the author took across meadows and parkland in the Midlands included the village of Berkswell, with what turned out to be a very remarkable church (LR139, P244792). It announced its oddity from the start. First glance showed a robust

Norman wall of startling red sandstone, onto which was tacked a porch like a little timber-framed cottage, with a priest's room above. Even more remarkable was the discovery of a staircase in among the pews leading down to a glorious vaulted twelfth-century crypt. It was like going through the door of a time machine.

One of the great appeals of any church is that one is never quite sure what one will find. Carvings, for example, often seem to reflect the whim of individual but anonymous masons. Gargoyles appear as mythical beasts, generally of the more ferocious kind, and other equally bizarre creatures can be found gazing down from ceilings or the pillars of capitals. Even more interesting are the depictions of recognisable and often very ordinary people to be discovered on pew ends and misericords, the little tilting half-seats found in choirs. These can be wonderful social documents in their own right. In Ludlow's magnificent church, for example, the misericords show many aspects of everyday life: a

Ludlow's mermaid misericord.

drunken tipster looks very unsteady on his feet as he fills his jug; a countryman sits snugly by the fire where a pot boils and sides of bacon hang behind him. But here the fabulous sit side by side with the realistic: on the far side of the choir a mermaid admires herself in a glass, flanked by very toothy dolphins. Often what seem to be outright pagan motifs appear: the Green Man, ancient symbol of fertility, occurs in a number of Somerset churches.

One of the finest walking areas in the country is the Quantock Hills, where one can combine a high-level walk along the open moorland to a summit overlooking the sea with a descent to one of the little villages that line up along the lower slopes. One of the most attractive is Crowcombe (LR181 ST141367) with its fifteenth-century Church House and the Church of the Holy Ghost with a tall red sandstone tower. But one has to go inside to find the extraordinary carvings at the ends of the sixteenth-century pews. One might wonder at what devout Christians were doing producing such images, which include the Green Man himself with vines bursting out of his mouth already laden with fruit. The Quantocks rise dramatically above the plain, and no less dramatic, if more modest in scale, is Brent Knoll, a shapely isolated hill with an Iron Age fort crowning the summit. The light effort required to climb it is rewarded by a bird's eye view over the surrounding wetlands, and from the top a path leads down to Brent Knoll church (LR182 ST335508). Here too one can find bench ends, carved in the fifteenth century, which if anything are even more remarkable than those of Crowcombe. There are some decidedly anti-clerical allegories here, showing a fox masquerading as an abbot, who fools his flock of birds until they are roused to rebellion by apes. The finale comes when the unhappy fox is stripped and hanged by the geese. Almost equally interesting is the splendid and colourful sixteenth-century memorial to John Somerset, elaborately carved and brightly painted, including a panel showing him rising from his coffin as the last trump is sounded from the clouds.

Memorials, whether inside or outside a church, can fascinate in many different ways. Some appeal because of the intricacy of their carvings, others because they are also records of the past life of the area. The great elaborate tombs of the rich and powerful tell us who were the great families that once dominated the whole area, but often it is the more humble stones that are the most revealing, depicting the ordinary life of the people. At Ashby St Mary in the heart of Norfolk Broadland, between the Waveney and the Yare (LR134, TG3202), the churchyard has two headstones side by side. They show George and Ann Basey, a sturdy farming couple, in country dress surrounded by their

North Cerney is a typically appealing Cotswold village with a no less delightful church. The grass of the churchyard is cropped, as it has been for generations, by sheep rather than a mower.

flock of geese. Here, held in stone, is the working life of a rural community a it was a century ago. Stones such as these are valuable documents, as revealing as drawings, paintings or even early photographs. Other churchyards show workers and the tools of their trade: some have elaborate inscriptions recounting the main details of the occupants' lives.

Over the years I have made it a rule never just to pass a village church by and to go inside whenever possible. Some will have little to say about the life of the community and not a great deal to catch the eye. The point is that until the door opens, one is never quite certain what to expect. The plainest church can hide the most delightful surprises.

Perhaps one needs less power of persuasion to suggest to many walkers that visit to the village inn or pub is also a good idea. Pub and church go together a lying at the very heart of a community, and the former often has its own rich associations and tales to tell. One of the sadder traits of recent years has bee name changes, often obliterating a useful hint to past history. The hamlet of Hulme End (LR119, SK1059) once boasted an inn called the Light Railway, reminder that the little Leek and and Manifold Light Railway ran nearby – only for a few years. The pub name tied railway to locale – and a short wall down the road reveals the old headquarters and engine shed, now a council roa

The extraordinary 12th-century crypt of Berkswell church where the vaulting sets up a complex rhythm, based on a ground plan of octagon and rectangles.

contrast to the underground glories of Berkswell, here is a church that leads the eye upwards. Angels
are down benignly from the roof of Southwold church.

epot. And there, too, is the trackbed of the old line, converted to footpath and
cleway. Village pubs are themselves often among the oldest village buildings,
uilt of local materials in local styles – and whereas it is generally possible only
are at the outside of houses, you are free to investigate the inside of the pub.
ften landlords are aware that customers might be interested in the history of
e area, and put up old photographs and prints – though not always with great
:curacy. One canalside pub which shall remain nameless has photographs of
cal' canal boats on the wall – though it seems very unlikely that Norfolk wher-
es, the sailing barges of the Broads, ever made it to the Rochdale Canal.

Most villages have grown and developed slowly over many centuries,
ough the pace of change has quickened very markedly in recent years. Even
, it is generally possible to see how that development occurred and recognise
e old patterns of settlement. Sometimes one is very conscious of a clear pat-
rn, where the village green forms the nucleus, ringed by houses, often strag-
ing away rather indiscriminately at the edges. Greens appear in many differ-
it parts of the country, but seem to crop up with remarkable frequency in
ast Anglia. One theory is that the green began as an area of wet, cloying soil,
nsuitable for crops, but available for common grazing, and as a result the vil-
ge would naturally spread out around the edge.

The village green at Hartest, surrounded by a jumble of houses of quite unrelated design. It still provides a community meeting place, this time for a village fete.

To take just one example, neither exceptionally grand nor unduly modest, Hartest in Suffolk (LR155, TL8352) sits in comfortable, undulating land well watered by a tributary of the little River Glem. Here is a good sized triangular village green, with church and inn at the apex. All around the green are houses of many different dates, some brightened by colour wash, others showing exposed timbers, the oldest with their upper floors jettied, projected out above the ground floor.

Other villages show different patterns of development, and there in some cases researchers have been able to come up with a rational explanation. The 'Harrowing of the North' began in 1069 when William the Conqueror sent his armed forces to the north of England with a mission to ruthlessly suppress resistance, which involved mass murder and the devastation of whole communities. The new Norman landowners then set about a process of rebuilding, and the old rather higgledy-piggledy patterns that followed centuries of random development gave way to a more formal approach. One such 'new' village was Wheldrake, near York (LR105, SE6845). Houses are strung out all along the main road through the village, and each one has a thin strip of land, or 'toft', running away behind it ending in a back lane. The two lanes curve round to meet at the church which occupies the dominant position at the top of the village. Later developments have not yet overwhelmed this old regularity. This is a pattern that can also be found in

many other regions – and in many cases the old back lanes still have the name, surviving into modern times, even when the village has grown out beyond them.

The two basic types of development are rarely seen in pure, unaltered form –
t is not even unusual to find them combined with houses clustered round a
green at one end and the rest opened out in a line with back lanes. Most villages,
after all, just grew almost organically and were not forced to adapt to any formal
design. Some, however, show signs of rigorous planning and conformity.
Walkers who follow the line of the River Thames become used to a pattern at
crossing points, whether at a bridge or where roads face each other across the
water, indicating an old ferry site. What you expect to find is a settlement of
some sort on either bank. Where the riverside path from Abingdon to Oxford
passes Radley (LR164 SU5398) there is just such a point, but across the river is
the parkland of Nuneham House. There was a village here, but the Harcourt
family demolished it when they wanted to create their park. A new model village
of strict uniformity, houses identical in style and set in neat blocks, was strung
out along the main road. Other great landlords, rather than remove the locals
out of sight altogether, preferred to include them in the scenery, building extrav-
gantly picturesque cottages for them to occupy, and none was more picturesque
than Blaise Hamlet on the outskirts of Bristol (LR172, ST5578).

ew things do more to establish the unique character and quality of a place than the use of local
materials. Age has only improved the patterns of worn stones round Shepton Mallet's market cross.

As in the previous picture, materials are all important. Cotswold stone has a richness and depth of colour no modern material can match, and where a Cotswold stone-slate roof is added the charm is complete.

One other type of planned village appeared in the eighteenth and earl nineteenth century, not as a result of a wish to beautify the scenery, but as par of the process of industrialisation. Early entrepreneurs often found it necessary when they established a new mill or factory, to build homes for the worker: Arkwright of Cromford and Strutt of Belper, early founders of the cotto industry, are famous examples. They created brand new villages in Derbyshire Some such settlements, notably Styal in Cheshire, have remained almost a they were when they were designed two centuries ago.

Each village has its own pattern, which relates to its own unique past an pattern of development, and many have their own little quirks and oddities a well, from often ornate village lock-ups to curious sundials. In short, a wa

:hrough a village can be just as interesting as a walk in the open fields. Villages ıre not often all of a piece. They are made up of grand houses and tiny cot-ages, very old buildings and very new. The difference between the first two is ikely to be a lot less than that between the latter. Until the Industrial Revolution, transport costs were so high that it made sense to use the nearest ıvailable building material for all houses, whether designed for the rich or for he poor. Exceptions could be made, notably in the case of churches where .tone was generally considered to be the most dignified material, and the most lurable. Otherwise local building materials ruled. It is this use of materials :hat gives towns and villages in Britain their immense diversity. We have)ecome very used to talking rather glibly about 'attractive places' without eally thinking what makes them attractive. Why do tourist flock to, for exam-)le, a Cotswold village? The answer lies to a large extent beneath the ground, ı the oolitic limestone of the region. Almost every settlement had its own .mall quarry, and the stone that emerged was soft and easily worked. The esult is a particular style of house, with high gables – no need to skimp on .tone – and fine detailing, such as the dripstones above finely carved mullioned vindows. Add to this formula a roof made out of 'stone slates' – an odd name, or these are not slates at all but slabs of limestone – and one has a house in vhich everything blends. Furthermore the stone itself weathers to a beautiful ich honey colour, which on a fine sunny day seems almost to glow with the .ght. Any Cotswold walk will bring such beauties into view, and there is no loubt that they add to the overall pleasure.

But there is rather more to it than that. Even if we do not always recognise :, there is a sense of unity about the whole area. The stone that can be ;limpsed at escarpment edges or in a small quarry, is the stone that divides up .elds as well as being the stone of barn, farmhouse and manor. Everything .olds together; nothing jars. It is only when other materials are introduced :hat there is a sense of an unwelcome presence in an otherwise harmonious ındscape. The builders of Cotswold villages did not set out to create pic-ıresque beauty: that grew up as a natural result of being true to the available ıaterials. The same holds for any area where stone is regularly used. The char-cter is determined by the materials. In the Yorkshire Pennines there is the ıme sense of unity that one finds in the Cotswolds, but of a very different haracter. Along the crests of hills, the dark masses of carboniferous sandstone, r millstone grit, rule a hard margin between land and sky. Again, the stone ıppears everywhere, but its dark colour and hard edges create an altogether ıore sombre picture than that of the soft, sunny stones of the Cotswolds. It is ıis, as much as the landscape, that gives a walk in Gloucestershire such a very ifferent character from a walk in the Pennines.

One could go on listing the great variety of stones available for building, from the granite of Cornwall in the west to the shiny flints of East Anglia. There is no need. Once one starts looking for the changes they quickly become obvious. But, of course, not all areas have stone available. The most popular alternative is brick, which has an understandably bad reputation, mainly because we think of the somewhat dull uniformity of the modern machine-made article. In earlier times, bricks were made out of local clay and fired in kilns where temperature control was at best haphazard. The result was bricks that varied immensely in colour, even if all were made from the clays of one small area. Time and again one finds walls of immense richness. Some of the loveliest effects are to be found in timber-framed buildings, where spaces between the timber can be filled by 'nogging'. The most common form of in-fill was the familiar wattle and daub, but brick provides a more permanent, better-wearing solution. And because the bricks do not have to support the

A beautiful example of a thatched Devon farmhouse. This was originally a longhouse, incorporating both byre and human living space under the same roof; designed to be practical, not picturesque.

An old timber-framed warehouse on Standard Quay, Faversham, that uses a huge variety of materials. Here the spaces between the timbers are filled with decorative brick nogging.

structure they can be arranged in a variety of different ways, not just level courses, but in herring bone patterns, or even rings. All this adds immensely to the richness of the structure. There are so many styles of building in Britain because there is such a wealth of different materials. There are walls of cob and walls of weather boarding, roofs of thatch and pantile, and so many more – and each change of material calls for a slightly different treatment from the builder. But one always has to remember that not all decisions are born out of necessity. Our ancestors were no different from ourselves. They wanted their houses to look attractive and, it has to be said, they wanted them to be admired by the neighbours as well. So a timber-framed house might have a good deal more timber than is strictly necessary, just to show the owner could afford it: a plain plaster wall might be transformed by pargetting, worked to form elaborate decorative patterns.

This whole process of looking at communities in the landscape can be brought right back to individual buildings. Even when one has looked at an area and gained an insight into the overall pattern of development, one can still find particular buildings which also have a story to tell. This is particularly true of rural areas, where many houses have been developed and even transformed over the years. A typical example is the longhouse, in which one end

The unselfconscious use of local materials has done more to create the beauty of the English village than any

Timber framing is a practical method of building where stone is not available. But at Lavenham, the wealthy piled it on to display their status to the world.

was a family living area, divided by a cross passage from the lower end, which would hold the working part of the household, including the kitchen, the dairy or even a byre for livestock. Long after such houses were unified to become conventional homes, the pattern survived – and in some areas, such as Devon, they are quite remarkably prolific. This is just one example from one region, and there is an immense wealth of regional variation. The same is true of purely functional farm buildings: anyone with a taste for elaborate woodwork should look up in the roof of some of our older barns.

These few notes are not intended as a guide to Britain's rich diversity of vernacular architecture, but more as a hint that it exists at all. For many of us who regularly walk in the countryside, the simple knowledge, however superficial, that there is this incredible diversity is in itself – literally – an eye-opener. Once one starts looking at buildings and their details one finds just how much there is waiting to be discovered. It is a process with no end. The landscape of these islands and the settlements large and small that have developed over the centuries have this immense variety, and a lifetime of walking and observing is not enough to come to terms with it.

There are some who are happy walking in just one small region, so that they get to know it ever more intimately, penetrating ever deeper below the more obvious attractions of surface beauty. Others prefer to range wide, noting the regional variations, comparing how different areas have come up with very different solutions to basically similar problems. I am one of the latter, but I have learned an immense amount from the former. It is up to each individual who feels the urge to get out on two feet and enjoy the countryside to decide which approach to adopt – or even to decide to settle for neither. All I have tried to show here is that in Britain we are blessed with a wonderfully rich scenery, full of subtle variations, and that the more one knows the greater one's enjoyment. Anyone can gain knowledge from reading a text book, but the walker gains both knowledge and pleasure from reading the best text book of them all, the countryside itself.

Further Reading

This is not intended to be a comprehensive list, rather suggestions for books that elaborate on the themes dealt with here. For those wishing to know more about a particular area, the series *The Making of the English Landscape* and *The Making of the Welsh Landscape*, edited by W. G. Hoskins and Roy Millward, which deals with individual counties and small regions is recommended. The following list roughly deals with subjects in the order in which they appear in this book.

W. G. Hoskins, *The Making of the English Landscape*, Hodder & Stoughton, 1977.

Richard Muir, *Shell Guide to Reading the Landscape*, Michael Joseph, 1981.

Ordnance Survey, *Land Navigation*.

Richard Muir, *History from the Air*, Michael Joseph, 1983.

Oliver Rackham, *The Illustrated History of the Countryside*, Phoenix House, 1997.

Christopher Taylor, *Roads and Tracks of Britain*, Dent, 1979.

Jacquetta Hawkes, *The Shell Guide to British Archaeology*, Michael Joseph, 1986.

Ordnance Survey, *Field Archaeology in Great Britain*, 5th edition, 1973.

Christopher Taylor, *Fields in the English Landscape*, Dent, 1982.

David Smurthwaite, *The Complete Guide to the Battlefields of Britain*, Ordnance Survey, 1984.

Oliver Rackham, *Trees and Woodland in the British Landscape*, Dent 1976.

Anthony Burton, *Canal Mania*, Aurum Press, 1993.

Anthony Burton, *The National Trust Guide to Our Industrial Past*, George Philip, 1983.

Trevor Rowley, *Villages in the Landscape*, Dent, 1978.

R. W. Brunskill, *Vernacular Architecture*, 2nd edition, Faber & Faber, 1978.

Alec Clifton-Taylor, *The Pattern of English Building*, Faber & Faber, 1972.

There is also an immense variety of very local books, too numerous to list, ranging from large learned tomes to small, cheap pamphlets. Often these are only available locally, to be found perhaps in the village shop, propped up between the cat food and the chocolate bars. They can, however, be informative, helpful in planning walks or useful in solving riddles met along the way. There are also a number of special interest maps available, of which the Ordnance Survey maps of Ancient Britain and Roman Britain are particularly useful for pinpointing interesting sites throughout the country.

Useful Addresses

British Trust for Ornithology, Beech Grove, Tring, HP12 5NR.

British Waterways, Willow Grange, Church Road, Watford, WD1 3QA.

CADW, Crown Buildings, Cathays Park, Cardiff, CF1 3NQ.

Countryside Commission, John Dower House, Crescent Place, Cheltenham, GL50 3RA.

Countryside Council for Wales, Plas Penrhos, Ffordd Penrhos, Bangor, LL57 2LQ.

English Heritage, 23 Savile Row, London, W1X 1AB.

English Nature, Northminster House, Peterborough, PE1 1HA.

Forestry Commission, 231 Corstorphine Road, Edinburgh, EH12 7AT.

Historic Scotland, Longmore House, Salisbury Place, Edinburgh, EH9 1SH.

Long Distance Walkers Association, 117 Higher Lane, Rainford, St Helens, WA11 8BQ.

National Trust, 36 Queen Anne's Gate, London, SW1H 9AS.

National Trust for Scotland, 5 Charlotte Square, Edinburgh, EH2 4DU.

Ordnance Survey, Romsey Road, Maybush, Southampton, SO16 4GU.

Ramblers Association, 1-5 Wandsworth Road, London, SW8 2XX.

Royal Society for Nature Conservation, The Green, Witham Park, Lincoln, LN5 7JR.

Royal Society for the Protection of Birds, The Lodge, Sandy, SG19 2DL.

Royal Society for the Protection of Birds, Cramond House, Kirk Cramond, Cramond Glebe Road, Edinburgh, EH4 6NS.

Scottish Natural Heritage, Battleby, Redgorton, Perth, PH1 3EW.

Scottish Youth Hostels Association, 7 Glebe Crescent, Stirling, FK8 2JA.

Sustrans, 35 King Street, Bristol, BS1 4DZ.

Youth Hostels Association, Trevelyan House, 8 St Stephen's Hill, St Albans, AL1 2DY.